Hooked on Fly-tying

Keith Draper

SHOAL BAY PRESS

First published in 1997 by
Shoal Bay Press Ltd
Box 2151, Christchurch

ISBN 0 908704 60 7

Cover photograph: Jon Hunter

Printed by Brebner Print Ltd, Auckland

Contents

INTRODUCTION

In 1973 I wrote two small instructional books, *Tie-a-Fly!* and *Nymphs for All Seasons*. For over ten years they have been out of print and I am continually being asked by anglers how they can obtain a copy. This is my answer. It is a new manual that covers a wide spectrum of fly-tying techniques, each explained step by step.

These days there is a huge range of tempting materials in the tackle shops. Some of the furs and plumages that were readily available when I tied my first flies 50 years ago are no longer available but there is a wealth of wonderful new products available for concocting exciting patterns.

Then there is the array of tools and mechanical aids designed to help the tier in the awkward stages of constructing a fly. When I started making my own flies I had a pair of scissors and a bodkin for a dubbing needle. I had no vice or hackle pliers. I held the hook in my fingers and taught myself to manipulate threads, flosses and feathers. When I had ruined a shop-bought fly by cracking off the barb through hitting the stones with my sloppy back casts I would carefully dissect it, unravelling the turns of thread, working out how it had been put together.

We kept bantams and other poultry, and, as I came from a shooting family, rabbit and hare skins were easy to come by, as were duck wings and flanks. It was the end of the war and some materials were impossible to obtain so I made do with what I could scratch up. I began by tying small wet flies, then larger Taupo-type flies. Eventually, as import restrictions were relaxed, I was able to obtain a vice and hackle pliers. I had already worked out how to make my own bobbin holder from wire, washers and a small bolt.

I have never regretted the time I spent making flies without all these modern aids: it gave me a good basic grounding in the art.

Then books on the subject started appearing and I was able to adopt and adapt new ideas and processes. What had started as a hobby eventually became a business. I became the owner of a trout fly factory and tackle distribution business. What with teaching staff to tie flies, and conducting fly-fishing schools for many years, I couldn't tell you how many people I have taught to make their own trout flies. A few found it was beyond them, others struggled on and mastered the art, and many found it was simplicity itself. With patience and care, most people are quite capable of turning out very good flies.

Catching a trout on a fly you have made yourself is a very satisfying business. Suddenly you have become the complete angler. You'll never forget the first trout that you deceived with a concoction of steel, fur and feather created by the skill of your own fingers.

TOOLS OF THE TRADE

Let us start by looking out the tools available to assist you in your task. You may be bewildered by the range, but remember that while all these gadgets may be useful at times you do not need to own them all. However, there are a few basic tools that you really should acquire. These are a good vice, fine-tipped scissors, a bobbin holder, hackle pliers and a dubbing needle.

Hooks

Hook sizes confuse many beginners. The larger the number, the smaller the hook. A number 2 is huge while a number 20 is very small. You will get used to this quite quickly.

Through my long association with the trout-fly industry I have handled literally millions of hooks and many other brands. Some were fine hooks but expensive. Others were liable to snap at the bend through over-tempering, while those that were under-tempered were soft and straightened very easily. For most of my life I have used Mustad hooks, which I have always found to be reliable. These days there are many other new brands available. Some, my friends tell me, are of excellent quality.

When selecting hooks, ensure that they are very sharp. Those that have been chemically sharpened have better points than those that have been sliced. A little work with a flat diamond hone will ensure that all of your hooks with sliced points are sharp.

If you are tying big lake and river flies you will need hooks with a limerick or sproat bend, sizes 2 to 8. They are less expensive if you buy them by the hundred. You will find that size 6 is the most popular.

For tying the smaller wet flies you will need a range from sizes 10 to 14. These hooks can also be used for tying nymphs but, for some of the patterns following, hooks with a slightly longer shank will be needed. These are classified as being 1x or 2x long. A packet each of number 12-2x and 14-2x will never go amiss, especially for tying damsel nymphs. Special curved hooks are available for tying caddis-type grubs. These are excellent. Numbers 12 and 14 are both handy sizes.

When tying dry flies you use hooks made with a finer wire, which are obviously lighter and more suited to the delicate floating patterns. You will need these from size 10 down to as small as you can handle. To a beginner size 14 is minute but with practice, and as your skill develops, you will be tempted to tie on the smaller sizes. For practical purposes you will seldom need to go any smaller than size 18, but if you become truly proficient you will find yourself trying your hand at minuscule flies tied on size 20 or even smaller.

As your fly tying progresses you will assemble a wide range of hooks. To start with buy some size 4s and 6s if you are tying the big lake flies, and some 10s and 12s for small wets and nymphs. You can expand on that range as you go.

Vice

A vice is perhaps the most important item of all. They range from simple models selling at a modest price up to expensive ones with quick-release jaws, revolving heads and other capabilities.

What should you buy? What can you afford – it's as simple as that. But be careful. Stay away from the flimsy pressed-metal models, the cheapest there is. Avoid them like the plague – they are just trouble. I know – I sold thousands of them. The basic chromed model with a knurled screw at the back of the jaw stem is simple, effective and moderately priced.

The quick-release type with a push-down, flip-up lever is excellent, except that it needs adjusting with the barrel-lock screw to modify the bite of the jaws according to the size of the hook being used.

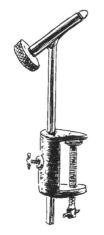

Vices: (far left a quick-release type, (left) a knurled-knob type and (above) a hand vice for streamside work.

Most of the cheaper vices are made from mild steel and if they are heavily used the metal in the jaws wears. The resultant distortion, caused by countless tightenings, means that eventually they will not hold smaller hooks properly. For the tier just wanting to make some flies for his own use this is no problem, but if you start to think in terms of making a few extra dollars when you have become proficient, then a vice with hard steel jaws is essential.

The Regal vice, an American model, has very hard jaws and a strong spring-loaded cam lock released by a side lever. A genuine Regal won't come cheap, and you should beware of cheap copies: they are a waste of money.

Scissors

These should be small, 90-100mm long, with fine sharp points and, most important, large finger holes. You may get by with a pair of nail scissors for a while but you'll find purpose- made ones are best.

Professional fly tiers hold their scissors in their hand all the time, hooked over their thumbs. The point of one of the blades is used for open-

11

ing up the feathers on Matuku-style flies to allow the tinsel ribbing to be wound through. You need to develop a certain amount of dexterity before you try this trick as it's very easy to spike yourself.

If you are into tying glo-bugs you will need a pair of shears. Cutting this yarn is heavy work for standard fly-tying scissors.

Bobbin Holder

Another indispensable item, these hold the spool of tying thread, keeping it under tension. Several types are available. They are all very useful but I prefer the model with a tube and a flared end. Try to get one with a hard steel tube, as soft metal wears and after a while the thread breaks, usually during the most critical part of the operation. The weight of the bobbin holder and the spool of thread will keep things in place when you need both hands to prepare materials for the next step in the tying plan.

Hackle Pliers

These gadgets really make things easy for the tier. They were designed for gripping the end of a hackle feather when winding it onto a fly, but they have other uses as well, one of which is to grip the end of oval tinsel when ribbing a streamer-type fly. They are available in several types and sizes. Some have scored metal jaws to aid gripping, while others have a little ribbed pad to prevent cutting the end of hackles when winding on. I find that a pair of medium-sized hackle pliers does most of the work I do.

Bodkin or Dubbing Needle

A must! These range from an ordinary darning needle stuck into the end of a piece of feather quill to one made of metal with a nicely checkered handle. Some have a hole in the tapered end for making half hitches. This is called a half-hitch bodkin.

The needle is used for opening up gaps in feathers during ribbing operations or pulling out hackle points that have become tangled under the thread and need rearranging. Fur bodies, especially those of nymphs, often need a bit of work with the needle to pull out spiky bits of fur around the thorax to give the fly a leggy look.

The needle is also handy for applying the odd drop or two of cement in critical places during a fly's construction.

Bobbin Threader

You'll need one of these to help get the thread down through the little narrow spout of the bobbin holder. It is also very useful if you are binding new rings onto one of your rods as it can be used to whip finish the binding and pull the end of the binding thread through.

Whip-finish Tools

These gadgets are one of those things which, if you are prepared to learn how to manipulate them, can be very handy. I use my fingers and the point of the bodkin to make whip-finished fly heads; others who have learnt to use them finish off a fly with a whip-finish tool in a few seconds.

Dubbing Twister

This gadget comprises a fine metal rod with a twisted loop on the end. The rod has a knurled butt section. The loop end is hooked into the tying thread, pulled down and the thread taken back to the fly. A quantity of fur used for making a dubbed body is teased along the double thread, the tool is twisted and the two strands of thread spin around each other, trapping the fur between them. This is explained more fully in the section dealing with making a dubbed fur body.

Tweezers

These can be useful for placing quill segments when making some of the nymph patterns. This can be tricky work.

Half-hitch Tools

These handy tools often come in sets: big ones for big flies and small ones for micros! They are good for making heads and for pushing hackle points back and out of the way when finishing off a fly.

Hackle Guards

One model of this tool comes as a bar with vari-

ous-sized holes for fly heads of different sizes. Large individual ones are excellent when making Muddler Minnows or flies with heads of deer hair. The guard enables you to push the deer hair back while the head is being finished. This way you end up with a nice even head without bits of straggly deer hair caught up in it.

Hair Stackers

This tool is designed to get the points of deer hair even, not the butt ends. On wings and tails made from bunches of deer hair, unless the points are shuffled they come out pretty straggly because that's the way deer grow their hair. So you cut a bunch of hair from the pelt, drop it down the throat of the tool, points first, then bang the gadget sharply on the table several times. You lay the tool on its side and take out the central tube. The hair will be lying inside and the points should all be pretty even. Now the chopped-off butt ends are uneven. You carefully select small bunches and extract them from the tube with the tip of the bodkin, then use them for winging and tailing deer-hair flies. You don't need this tool to make Muddler heads or clipped deer-hair bodies.

BODY MATERIALS

Chenille

For the large flies you will need a range of chenilles. These are bought in small packets or wound onto cards. Yellow, orange, red, green, olive and black are the main colours. Then there are the bright fluorescent colours, used for tying Dappled Dogs and Tongariro patterns. Chenille is a wonderful body material and they are simple to use.

Floss

There was a time when a range of floss silks was an important part of every fly tier's equipment. They were used for making the bodies of salmon flies, small wets and dry flies. Except for a few dry fly patterns they are seldom needed these days. For a start, I would suggest a small spool of black, primrose, red and olive for making the bodies of some of the more standard dry flies and some nymphs. Later on you can buy every shade on offer if you wish.

Fur

Hare fur and rabbit fur are both excellent materials for making 'dubbed' bodies. So is possum fur, particularly the long black hair from its tail. This is quite suitable for fly tails but it tends to have a kink in it that puts off tiers who are used to seeing tails of straight squirrel hair. Believe me, the difference is only cosmetic: the trout certainly don't discriminate!

Squirrel tails are still available for tying the tails of standard lake flies such as the Mrs Simpson and Fuzzy Wuzzy. Muskrat fur makes wonderful nymphs and Granny's old fur coats and stoles may be a source of this material.

Some furs, such as seal fur and mohair, are now either banned or unprocurable. Don't worry, there are plenty of substitutes available. Polydub, Antron, Speckly yarn and other synthetic yarns all serve well. Wherever you come across an old dressing that gives a component that is no longer available do not panic: there will be a substitute to take its place. Ask at your local tackle shop and they will direct you toward the appropriate material.

Tinsel

Modern mylar tinsels are far superior to metallic tinsels, which tarnish easily. You will need a selection of flat tinsels in gold and silver, and oval tinsels for ribbing. If you do have metallic tinsels they will not tarnish if you keep them in a screw-top jar with a pinch of camphor crystals.

Besides their use in making bodies, several mylar-related materials are now used for adding flash to the wings of some streamer patterns. Flashabou and Krystelhair are the brand names for two types of material. It comes in bunches of fine metallic strips that are extremely flexible and have a high reflective flash factor. A few strands tied in at the head of a streamer fly gives added flash as it moves through the water, suggesting the struggles of a wounded smelt or fry.

These materials are available in a whole range of colours, with pearl flash being the most popular.

Quill Bodies

The long strands from a peacock's tail feather are used for making the quill bodies of dry flies. The herl is stripped from the strand, which is wound on to form a segmented body. An artificial substitute is a plastic material called Swannundaze. It comes in a variety of colours and may be heated and stretched to downsize it. The central spine of a cock neck hackle feather stripped of its barbs will also make a quill body. These may be dyed.

Poultry Hackles

The most commonly used feathers are the neck hackles from domestic poultry, with the hackles from finely bred cock birds being highly prized. The small feathers from the top of the neck are used for tying dry flies, while the larger hackle feathers from the shoulder are used for tying streamer and Matuku-type flies. The long feathers over the bird's back, or saddle, are useful for tying larger types of dry flies and also saltwater flies.

All of these poultry hackles come in a range of natural colours: white, cream, black, white with black centre (badger), dark natural red, light red, ginger, honey, red with black centre (dark furnace), ginger with black centre (light furnace), blue dun, honey dun, white with black bars and flecking (grizzle), barred light and dark red (honey grizzle), barred white and red (cree) and other mixed colours which defy description and are collectively known as variants. Then there are the dyed colours: bright yellows, scarlets, greens, and grizzle-dyed olive for tying Green Orbits.

A neck of hackles from the finest bird will cost a lot of money as it has been specially bred and fed for several years until it reached its prime. It will probably be a Metz or Hoffmann-bred bird, from the US. If you want to tie top-quality dry flies you should consider investing in one or two necks. If you are happy to settle for tying good-quality dries then an Indian neck will serve you well. These little necks, in the better quality, will carry quite a lot of fine hackles suited to the job. You might need to use two hackles where one from an American neck would suffice.

Chinese cock necks tend to have soft hackles. You will find that some will tie quite passable dry flies, but the strength of the Chinese neck is the beautiful larger hackles it produces, which make excellent streamer and Matuku-style flies. Chinese necks, which are quite big, are usually about the same price as the smaller Indian ones.

The large Chinese hackles are sold in strings. They are plucked from the bird, sorted, graded for length, then individually strung on a thread about a metre long. They start off at about 10cm long, tapering off to 5cm. Strings can be obtained graded either larger or smaller, cut into sections and packeted.

These long cock neck hackles can become twisted or bent but don't throw them away! Twisted feathers can be straightened out by holding them in the steam of a boiling jug or kettle. Bundle up the discards, tie them around the base of the stems with thread, then hold them with tongs over the steam, turning them around. Nearly all will straighten out and when dried and fluffed up they will be very usable.

Other Plumage

Duck feathers are useful, especially the grey speckled breast and flanks of a mallard drake. Duck wings are indispensable. The flight feathers are used as a supply of snips for winging dry flies. The white-tipped speculae feathers from a mallard wing are used for winging Peverils and Heckam Peckams.

Paradise duck feathers are great. The speckled plumage from the male drake makes Lacemoths or provides excellent side feathers when tying big lake flies. The brown secondary feathers from both the drake and hen are well suited to making the wing cases of Brown Beetle flies. The fine feathers from around the heads of these birds are full of grease and are excellent for winging no-hackle-type Spent Spinners.

The ruddy brown breast feathers of a shoveller drake make Brown Killers, while pukeko feathers are used for tying large lake night flies. Cock pheasant plumage is highly prized. The bronze and green rump feathers are used for tying Mrs Simpsons, while the tail feathers are the prime ingredient for the Pheasant Tail Nymph.

Quail plumage makes excellent flies. The side flanks from the brown quail make an acceptable substitute for woodcock plumage and can be used to tie Lord's Killers. The white- centred body plumage from a Californian quail is a substitute for jungle cock side cheeks, used in the larger streamer-type flies.

Swan and goose flight quills and secondary flight feathers also have a use. As well as serving as a winging material they are the source of biots, used for tying legs into stonefly-type nymphs.

The fly tier who is also a shooter can obtain most of this material during the season. If you are lucky enough to come by a wild farm turkey then a long supply of valuable materials is assured. In addition to the tail and wing feathers there are the fluffs around the legs and posterior, which are known as turkey marabou. Dyed, these are the main ingredients of that top fly the Woolly Bugger.

English grey partridge plumage is becoming difficult to obtain but if the opportunity arises seize it. The grey speckled breast makes great leg hackles when tying nymphs, while the brown plumage is great for tying March Brown wets or Hare and Partridge nymphs. Grouse plumage is another handy import. It is not as difficult to obtain as partridge but the worldwide demand for plumage means that it will be at a premium one day.

Peacock herl is the basis of many flies. Fortunately it is still relatively easy to obtain but this might not always be the case, so if you have the opportunity to stock up do so. There is a surprising number of feral peacocks in New Zealand but most of the herl sold in sport shops comes from India and Asia.

Hair

Deer hair is used a lot in flies these days so you'll need some in your kit. Red deer hair is not very useful as it is flat and hard, except for a narrow strip around the rump known as the caudal disc. Hair from sika deer is better but also a bit hard, except again for the caudal disc. It makes great tails for dry flies.

Part of the pelt from a fallow deer is better, especially the rump and the rear flanks, but the best of the lot is hair from an American white tail deer. They are found in New Zealand, mainly on Stewart Island, but they are so prized that most hunters tend to treat the skin as a trophy. They don't seem interested in cutting off a piece and donating it to the science of fly tying!

Elk or wapiti pelts produce excellent hair, invaluable for tying up Elk Sedges or making up bodies of Irresistibles and Cicadas, and good for the head of that great pattern the Muddler Minnow.

Goat hair is useful for making fly tails, especially black hair, but it needs to be from a young animal, not a stinking old billy! White goat hair makes good streamer hair flies, especially when used fly fishing for kahawai or kingfish.

Bucktail from deer is used for making Bucktail Streamers. It can be either used in natural white or brown or dyed.

White calf tail is used mainly for winging dry flies and is an essential ingredient of the popular Royal Wulff.

Artificial Hair

Modern industry has come up with many fibres that are used in the fly-fishing industry. Fishair is a brand name for a wide range of artificial hairs available in natural whites and browns as well as grizzled or dyed any colour you can think of.

These can be mixed with furs and feathers to give added body or dash to a fly, or used as a complete substitute for bucktail, bear fur, yak tail or whatever takes your fancy.

Then there is Nylo-tail, a fluorescent hair-like material which glows under ultra-violet light. It is used extensively for saltwater jig flies but ties up well on freshwater patterns as well.

Egg Yarn or Glo-bug Yarn

This brightly coloured yarn was first used on the salmon and steelhead rivers of the US, where it was used to imitate bunches of salmon eggs. The Glo-bug and its derivative, the Muppet, are now part of the New Zealand angling scene. It has been agreed by the authorities that the Glo-bug complies with the definition of a trout fly. The yarn makes excellent bodies for standard flies and, treated with silicone, it is also used for making floating indicators for nymph fishing.

Jungle Cock Eyes

These feathers were used as a feature of practically all the old salmon and streamer fly patterns. Then their importation was prohibited by most countries as a conservation measure, as the demands of the world fly-tying market were leading toward the extinction of the bird in its native Asia. But the bird is now grown in captivity and these domesticated capes with their enamelled feathers are available – at a price. Substitutes can be made by applying dabs of acrylic paint onto black hen hackles, but I have already suggested elsewhere the use of hackles from Californian quail, which are readily available in this country.

Threads

To my way of thinking there is only one really good tying thread and that is Mono-cord: a flat yarn available in a variety of sizes and colours. You can also buy a waxed form. The waxing is to facilitate the spinning or dubbing of body furs onto the thread when making nymph and fly bodies but it does make a mess of the spigot on the bobbin holder. I prefer to use regular thread and wipe a bit of tying cement onto it to help the fur to stay in place.

In general I do not like nylon thread as it stretches when being used. It certainly holds materials to the hook but when the fly is finished and the thread snipped it has a tendency to return to its original length, slip back under the whip finish or hitches and the fly comes undone. I like nylon for tying large saltwater flies, though.

Head Paints and Cements

'Does it come in a bottle with a brush? No? Well, I don't want it!' Call it marketing or an example of human foible, but if head paints and cements are in bottles without a brush the buying public doesn't want them.

But in fact the brush is totally useless for applying cement to small fly bodies and heads. Here is my way. You push a darning needle through a cork and use that to apply your cement and head paints. Believe me, it's far better suited to working with flies than any brush. But I gave up trying to drum this bit of simple logic into the skulls of sporting retailers up and down the length of this fine fishing country of ours. I gave in and my company duly sent out thousands of bottles of cement and head paints with a totally useless brush in them. Here endeth the lesson.

The cement is a vital part of the tier's armoury. It can be used to hold the body together and stop it from skewing around the hook shank, as well as being applied to the head to stop it unravelling and coming to pieces. When making small flies and nymphs cement is quite sufficient for sealing and finishing the head, but on larger lake flies and streamers black lacquer makes a nice shiny head. This may not increase its trout appeal but will certainly increase its aesthetic appeal. If you tie many Taupo Tigers or Yellow Ladies you will need a bottle of red. Some like to use grey paint to finish off the heads of smelt patterns such as the Grey Ghost and the Doll Fly.

Many of the bigger flies, especially the minnow- and smelt-suggesting patterns, are improved with the addition of an eye, for which a bottle of white or yellow lacquer will be needed. A dot of this is put on the finished head of a fly then when it's dry a small dot of black is placed in the centre to represent the pupil. A round toothpick with the tip cut off square is perfect for this job. Then the whole lot is given a coat of clear cement. It will end up a really classy fly!

You will also need a bottle of thinners because cement and head paints tend to evaporate and thicken very easily. A small drop of thinners added now and then will help prevent this. Make sure all caps are replaced tightly when not in use.

Wire

Fine gold and silver wire is used for ribbing small flies. Copper wire should be in every fly tier's kit: it makes an excellent ribbing for nymphs and can also be used for weighting the underbodies of some nymph patterns. You can buy it in spools from the tackle shop or from workshops specialising in rewinding armatures, coils and other electrical gizmos. These places often have bulk spools with unusable tail lengths on them. Another source is power flex, which can be stripped to obtain the fine copper wire cores.

Lead

This is essential for weighting the bodies of nymphs and can be bought in spools. Some buy lengths of lead-cored trolling line and tease out the lead wire centre. The lead seal wraps from the top of bottles of spirit can be flattened and cut into strips, as can sheet lead of the type used by plumbers for making weatherproof flashings.

Much has been recorded regarding the health risks of working with lead. I personally believe that the risk inherent in using lead to weight a few flies is minimal. Nevertheless, you should always wash your hands thoroughly after working with lead, and any who would prefer not to do so could employ copper wire instead. Of course this is not as heavy and to obtain the sink weight of a lead-weighted number 10 hook it may be necessary to go to a number 8 if you are using copper.

Professional fly-tier, fishing guide and tackle dealer Mike Stent at work.

The fly-tier's bench

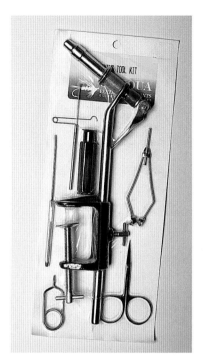

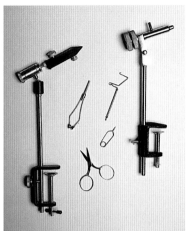

ABOVE: Essential tools: vices, bobbin holder, whip finish tool, hackle pliers, scissors.

LEFT: Beginner's tool set: vice, bobbin holder, scissors, hackle pliers, bodkin, whip finish tool, hair stacker

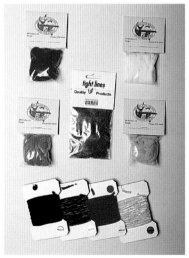

Chenilles and dyed dubbing fur

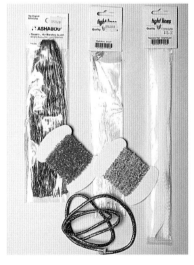

Artificial materials: Flashabou, Nylo hair, sparkle chenille, mylar tubing.

Hen cape, jungle cock cape and assorted cock neck feathers

Grizzle saddle and natural red cock neck

Hare's mask, black rabbit pelt and olive-dyed maribou

Natural bucktail, dyed deer hair, natural deer hair

GETTING ORGANISED

Storing your Materials

I have seen some very elaborate methods of storing fly-tying materials. A writing desk is probably the best if you have room for it. Others just use old shoeboxes and the like. Whatever method you do use, remember that there is a pestiferous enemy just waiting for you to turn your back so it can begin destroying your treasures. No, I am not talking about your neglected spouse, I am referring to that dratted insect the carpet moth.

The larvae of this horrible little beast will turn feathers and fur into dust and insect droppings in no time flat. Your feathers and furs must be protected against it in airtight canisters, metal or plastic. Pop some moth crystals, naphthalene or camphor in the container in case some eggs are already on the materials when you store them. Ignore this advice at your peril: you may go to get out your expensive plumage one day and find that many dollars worth of priceless feathers have been ruined.

Setting up to Tie

Regardless of where you work you will need good light, preferably diffused. Sunlight is better coming through netting than unfiltered; direct sunlight is too harsh. An eye-shade is good if you are working in semi-direct sunlight. A simple peaked cotton baseball-type cap will do – try one, it really helps.

If you work at night you will need a good lamp, preferably one with an extendable stand. You can adjust it so that it shines directly onto your vice. Once again you may find that an eye-shade helps. If you are right handed you should have the light coming in on your right shoulder; left-handed tiers work in reverse.

You are going to make a mess. If you are in your den or out in the garage that's okay, but if you are working at the kitchen table you had better take care or you won't be welcome there again. Set up your vice and then on the right-hand side (if you are right handed) tape a paper or plastic bag to the front edge of the table. When you need to trim things you just turn a little to the right and do your snipping and trimming over the waste bag. All the bits and pieces are popped into it and don't have to be swept up off the floor and carpet. You are earning brownie points already!

It also pays to lay a few sheets of newspaper around. Remember all those bottles of cement and lacquer – if an open one falls onto the floor it can be extremely difficult to clean up, especially if it lands on the carpet. It can be just as disastrous on vinyl as the solvent can remove the pattern and leave horrible bumps. Take care!

A small block of florist's styrofoam is ideal for sticking the points of finished flies into while the heads dry.

Selecting Hackles from a Cape

While you can buy packets of strung hackles for tying streamer and Matuku-style flies, and small packets of selected dry and wet fly hackles, many prefer to buy a cape, or neck of feathers. These will be from either a rooster or a hen. Let us take a look at a rooster (cock) cape, Fig. A.

Illustrated are four cock neck hackles. Number 1 comes from the bottom of the cape, as indicated. These are fine for tying the larger-sized Matuku and streamer flies. Number 2 hackles come from around the middle of the cape and are excellent for tying Matuku flies in the smaller sizes.

A number 3 hackle is used for tying large dry flies and very small streamers.

Hackles used in tying top-quality dry flies come from the top of the cape: number 4. These feathers should be narrow with very little web.

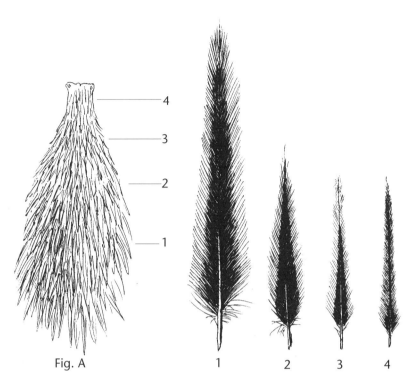

Fig. A   1   2   3   4

What is web? Take hackles 1, 2 and 3. Notice the dark tapering centre of the hackle? That is the web. It is soft while the shiny ends of the barbs are stiffer. In a good dry-fly hackle there is little or no web. If the small hackles from the top of the cape have a web down their centres then your dry-fly cape is not top quality and its hackles will not make top flies. The barbs will be soft and won't support the weight of the fly on the surface of the water.

That is how you decide whether a cape is a good-quality dry-fly one before you buy it. If the small fine hackles at the top have no web (see no. 4) it is a quality cape, so long as the feathers are in good condition, unbroken at the tips and with a good sheen.

If you just want large hackles for tying streamer flies the quality of the cape is not so important. If a cape lacks the quality dry-fly hackles the rest will probably make excellent larger flies and you

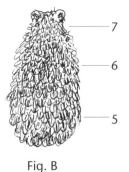

Fig. B   5   6   7

can use the smaller ones for tying small wets and nymphs. The cape should cost you a lot less than a truly top-grade one. There is always room for some cheaper capes in your range of materials.

Hen's capes, Fig. B, come cheaply and the feathers are soft – ideal for small wet flies and nymphs. The smallest, number 7, used when tying little patterns, comes from the top of the cape. The middle-sized one, number 6, comes from the middle of the neck. These are ideal for flies tied on number 10 or 8 hooks.

The larger hen hackle, number 5, comes from the bottom of the cape. These can be used on very big wet flies or dragon-sized nymphs, or for tying short-tailed Matuku-style flies.

Cock and hen capes are both available in a range of colours: black, natural reds, furnace, honey grizzle, grizzle, badger, blue dun and all the dyed colours.

BASIC TECHNIQUES

The instructions in this manual are for right-handed people. If you are left handed you will need to reverse the instructions. I can tell if a fly has been made by a left-handed tier the minute I set eyes on it as all the windings have an opposite slant.

Placing the Hook in the Vice

Every hook has a sharp point and if you look at the illustrations you will note that the hook is placed in the jaw of the vice so that the bend is firmly grasped, leaving the point exposed. This point will occasionally catch on the tying thread as it is being wound around the shank, causing it to break. This is a great nuisance, but can be avoided with care.

One way to avoid the risk is to place the hook in the vice jaws with the point fully enclosed. However, with some of the smaller fine-wired hooks this is inviting them to break, and when tying on larger hooks it is not always possible to enclose the point within the vice jaws. If it is safe to have the point locked in the jaws do so, but remember the above advice.

Right-handed people place the hook in the vice with the eye of the hook on their right.

Winding on the Thread

1

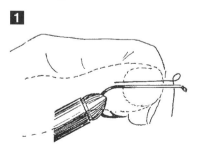

Now it is time to begin winding on the thread. Start off by laying the tail end of the thread along the hook shank. Hold it in place with the fingers of your left hand (Fig. 1).

29

Wind the thread back toward the bend of the hook, wrapping it over the tail of the thread. When the hook shank is fully wrapped it should look like the one in Fig. 2.

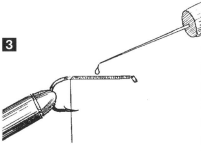

This is how all flies are started. It is a good idea now to wipe a touch of cement along the top of the shank (Fig. 3). This will set quickly, helping to bond the base of thread to the hook and making for a strong fly that will not twist around the shank of the hook.

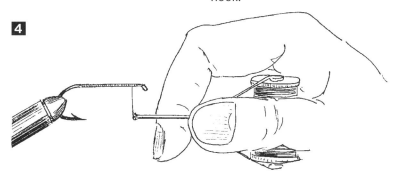

When binding the thread around the hook shank, at all times keep the thread as short as you can. If you allow too much thread to draw off, the bobbin will hit on the table. Hold the bobbin and use as illustrated in Fig. 4, with only a short length between the bobbin spigot and the hook shank.

If the thread draws off the bobbin too easily you need to increase the tension. This is accomplished by removing the spool of thread from the bobbin holder and bending the spring legs in slightly. If the tension is too tight, the reverse exercise applies.

Winding on Hackles

1

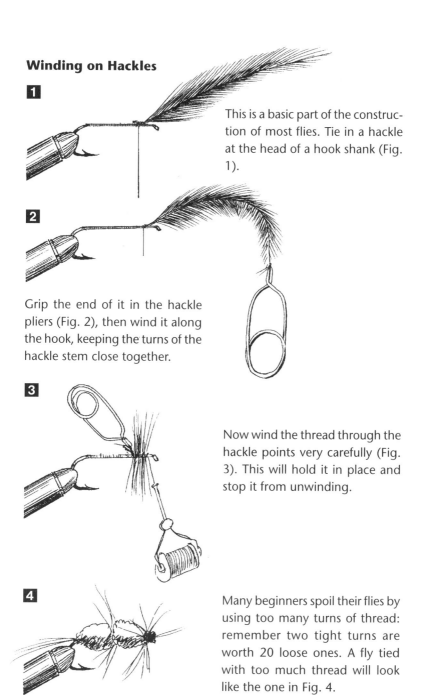

This is a basic part of the construction of most flies. Tie in a hackle at the head of a hook shank (Fig. 1).

2

Grip the end of it in the hackle pliers (Fig. 2), then wind it along the hook, keeping the turns of the hackle stem close together.

3

Now wind the thread through the hackle points very carefully (Fig. 3). This will hold it in place and stop it from unwinding.

4

Many beginners spoil their flies by using too many turns of thread: remember two tight turns are worth 20 loose ones. A fly tied with too much thread will look like the one in Fig. 4.

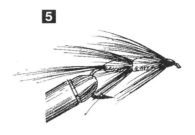

If you use a moderate number of turns it should look like the one in Fig. 5.

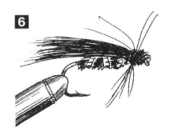

Another mistake is to take the body materials too far along the hook shank. This means you end up with an oversized head, usually blocking up the eye of the hook (Fig. 6).

You need a few millimetres of empty shank to execute a well-balanced head (Fig. 7).

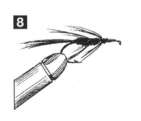

Too much space and you will end up with the other extreme – a long gangly head, what we call a goose-necked fly (Fig. 8).

Dubbing a Fly Body

Throughout this book you will find patterns that call for a body of dubbed fur. This is literally a 'pinch' of fur spun onto the tying thread. Some people buy little gadgets that help during this process. Others use a separate thread and double it. The two strands are held separate with a spreader while fur is distributed along the threads. Then the two strands are twisted together, entrapping the pieces of fur so you end up with a rope of dubbed fur.

People will tell you that this is the best way to make dubbed bodies. It is effective, but I believe that the simple way I use, the old traditional method, is as good as any.

The first mistake made by most beginners is that they take too much fur to start off with (Fig. 1).

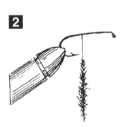

Note that I always use the term 'a pinch of fur' (Fig. 2). That is the first secret.

The second one is to make the tying thread tacky so that the fur sticks to it. You can use wax or cement for this. I use the same cement I put on the heads or use for strengthening the bodies. You just need a small wipe with your needle along the thread. Don't use much.

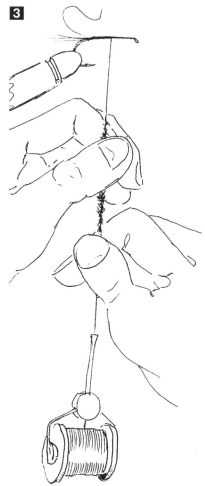

3

Then roll the pinch of fur around the thread with the fingers of your left hand while the other holds the thread taut. You spin the fur by drawing the forefinger of the left hand down along the back of your thumb as illustrated in Fig. 3.

Make it into a taper, then, using carefully regulated turns, wind it on to form the fly or nymph body. If you need more fur, just add another small pinch. Avoid clumps of fur or you will end up with a lumpy and untidy body.

Ribbing tinsel wound onto the body (see individual pattern instructions) will give extra reinforcement and hold the fur in place.

You will be using this technique a lot, especially when making nymphs, so I suggest an evening at the vice just practising dubbed bodies. It is a knack that you'll achieve with practice and care.

When making Hare and Copper nymphs you will learn to tease out the long black-tipped guard hairs and keep them for making the rough leggy-looking thorax of the fly, while the softer underfur is ideal for making the abdomen.

Making a Deer-hair Body

To spin on a deer-hair body, cut off a bunch of deer hair, lay it across the hook shank and take two loose turns of the thread over it (Fig. 1).

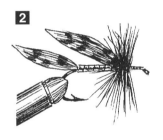

Let the hair go as you pull and tighten the thread. The hair will splay out and spin around the hook shank (Fig. 2).

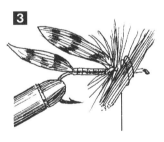

Tie in another bunch (Fig. 3).

Push the hair back to keep it tight. Spin on enough bunches to fill up the rest of the hook. Place a half-hitch tool over the eye of the hook and push the hair back, making several half hitches to keep the hair in place.

Snip off the thread and apply a generous drop of cement. We are now ready to start clipping (Fig. 4).

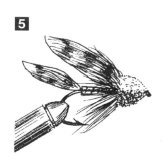

5

Remove the fly from the vice and squeeze the hair along the sides. Clip it to shape: one cut on top; one cut below. Then shift your grip and squeeze the hair with your fingers above and below the hair, and clip along the sides. Make these cuts at an angle as though you are trying to form a cone. Leave some of the back hairs intact.

You will have made four main cuts, one above, one below and one on each side. A bit more trimming will round it off and you should have something resembling the fly in Fig. 5.

Finishing off a Fly Head

This operation may be accomplished with a whip finish or by half hitching.

1

For a whip finish you can use a whip-finish tool, which comes complete with instructions. With this method the tail of the thread is pulled back under several securing turns, exactly the same way a rod binding is finished off (Fig. 1).

The half-hitch tool is a very useful implement that speeds up the half-hitch operation. Some dubbing needles have the end of the handle turned down and counter sunk, making a combination tool. The end of a large quill also makes an excellent half-hitch tool when tying small flies. Even the end of a used ballpoint pen with the innards removed is quite useful.

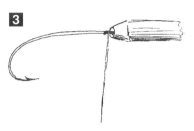

The thread is wound around the end of the tool as shown in Fig. 2.

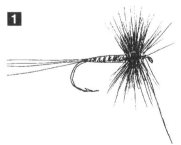

The hole on the end of the tool is then slipped over the eye of the hook and the loop of thread slipped down around the head of the fly and pulled tight (Fig. 3).

If you use half hitching to finish off a head (a practice frowned upon by some tiers), you need to make several as insurance against the end of the thread coming loose. Run them back with the last hitch at the back of the head. When trimming the thread leave a tag of about a millimetre and carefully apply some cement to hold the head together and prevent the stitches slipping.

Which method do I use? I have half hitched most of my flies all of my fly-tying life, but I have always used a whip finish for large flies, and especially for saltwater flies in which heavy nylon thread is used.

See 'Head Paints and Cements' in Chapter 2 for details of the finishing paintwork.

Other Uses for a Half-hitch Tool

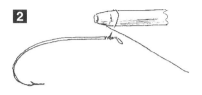

When finishing a dry fly, or even big wet flies, the hackle may have bits sticking out all over the place. Those jutting forwards make achieving a neat head difficult (Fig. 1).

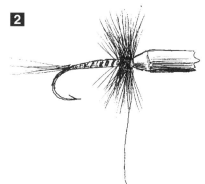

2

The half-hitch tool soon puts these unruly hackle barbs in their place. Push them back with the tool, then, to keep them in position, throw on a couple of hitches. This tool can also be used to effect when building heads of spun deer hair, for pushing the hair back along the hook shank and compacting it to form a full, well-packed head.

We are now ready to start. Let's begin by tying a large and relatively simple pattern that embodies many of the disciplines used in tying all flies.

CRAIG'S NIGHT TIME

MATERIALS

Limerick or sproat hook, size 4-8
Thick piece of scarlet wool
Black chenille

Silver oval tinsel
Blue pukeko breast feathers
Jungle cock eyes or yellow cock
    hackle barbs

This is an easy fly to tie and is the pattern I have always started new pupils on.

Set the hook in the vice, wind around the shank with thread, then tie in a tuft of bright red wool. Next you tie in the tinsel and then the black chenille (Fig. 1).

Wind the chenille carefully along the hook shank, stopping at least 5mm short of the eye to leave enough clear shank for making the head. Don't make the normal beginner's mistake and wind the chenille right up to the eye or you will end up with a horrible-looking creation with a fat, lumpy, untidy head. Neither do you want an overlong or goose-necked head: leave about a 4-5mm space.

You then wind the tinsel along in evenly spaced turns and secure at the head. Make a couple of half hitches to hold things together and trim off the ends (Fig. 2).

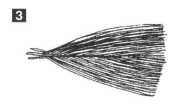
3

Take three or four evenly matched blue breast feathers from a pukeko (substitute plumage can be bought from fly tying shops), trim them and lay them on top of one another (Fig. 3).

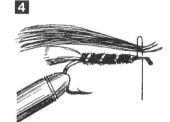
4

Place them on top of the fly body, keeping them in place with a couple of moderately firm turns (Fig. 4).

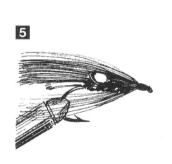
5

Take a firm grip on the bobbin, pulling the thread tight, then with the finger and thumb of the other hand pull the sides of the feathers down. The lower filaments of the feathers now drape low along the sides. Hold them in place and wind the thread around to secure them. Trim off the butts and secure (Fig. 5).

You may finish this fly by tying in jungle cock feathers on the side, or, as they used to do 50 years ago, tie a single jungle cock on top, right in the middle. These days many tie the Craig's with a tuft of yellow hackle barbs on top: it's your choice. Either way, it's a good night fly and a good pattern to learn from.

BLACK PHANTOM

MATERIALS

Limerick or sproat hook, size 2-8
Black squirrel tail
Black chenille

Silver oval tinsel
Black pukeko plumage
Jungle cock feathers (optional)

This fly is an easy pattern to tie. Some like to tie this pattern with the four feathers tied atop the body in the manner of a Craig's Night Time. It is a matter of personal choice: either way it's a top night fly.

Secure the hook in the vice, whip on the thread, then tie on a small bunch of black squirrel tail (Fig. 1). Avoid the mistake made by many beginners of using too much tail hair. Better to add a little more if it looks a bit ratty than have a big lump that looks like a shaving brush.

Let a drop of cement soak into the butts of the tail, then tie in a strip of tinsel and the end of the chenille. On a larger hook, say a number 2 or 4, you should not need more than 50mm of both. If making a fly on a smaller hook 30-40mm will be enough.

Wipe a drop of cement along the hook shank then wrap the chenille, making careful even turns toward the eye. Leave a gap between the end of the chenille and the eye: about 8mm for a larger fly, 5mm for a smaller.

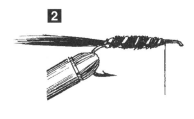

When the body has been formed, secure the end of the chenille with a couple of tight turns of the tying thread and trim. Then take the end of the tinsel in the pliers and wind it along in nice evenly spaced turns. Secure it with the tying thread and trim. Your fly body and tail are now complete (Fig. 2).

Take four black feathers from a pukeko's flank or back. If the genuine article cannot be obtained, duck plumage dyed black is obtainable from fly-tying shops. Match your feathers and trim them so that they are all reasonably equal in size. Strip the fluff off the ends of the feathers.

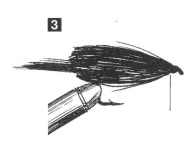

With care, and **using moderately firm turns**, secure a feather to each side, placed so that they reach just beyond the bend of the hook. Then repeat the process. You will now have two feathers on each side of the body. Now make several tight turns and half hitch (Fig. 3).

If you wish to add dash to this handsome pattern you can add cheeks of jungle cock feathers. Finish off the head, secure and trim it, then paint it black (Fig. 4).

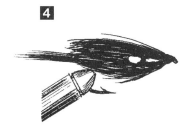

BOOBY FLY

MATERIALS

Limerick or sproat hook, size 2-6
Small styrofoam balls
Nylon mesh or polythene plastic
  sheeting

Olive marabou
Gold tinsel, fine
Olive chenille
Olive grizzle hackle

This tie is based on the Olive Woolly Bugger. The Booby aspect comes with the use of the foam balls as eyes. These are floats because booby flies are designed to be fished just above the bottom on a sinking line. They are cast out and after the line has reached the bottom, the lure, because of its in-built flotation, will rise in the water.

It is a virtually snag-proof fly, unless you strike a tangle of sunken branches! It is an ideal pattern for working over sandy or gravel bottoms.

An all-black version of this pattern is a popular night fly, used around stream mouths.

The balls can be bought from some tackle shops or from a hobby shop. They are used for stuffing bean bags or as fill in packaging around fragile items. Your local glass and crockery shop might have them in its rubbish bin. You need two for each fly (Fig. 1).

Place each one in a square of mesh, taken from a pair of women's tights, for instance (ensuring they are not occupied at the time). Alternatively you can cut a square from a plastic supermarket-type bag. That way you can use red, green, black or any coloured plastic you come across that takes your fancy. It must be of a light gauge and strong. Cut out your piece, about 30mm square, and place the foam ball on it (Fig. 2).

Pull the ends together so that the ball is encapsulated (Fig. 3).

Now whip two of these balls to the shank of the fly hook. Cut off any excess plastic or mesh, then cement the thread (Fig. 4).

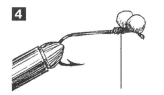

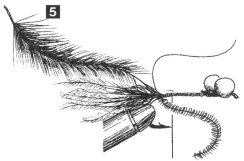

From here we follow the Woolly Bugger recipe. Tie in the tail of marabou, then a strand of tinsel, then a piece of chenille and the tip end of the hackle (Fig. 5).

6

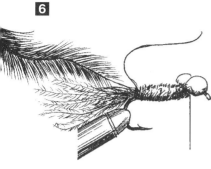

Wind on the chenille body (Fig. 6).

7

Now wind on the hackle. Secure it with the tinsel, which is counter-rotated to the hackle stem. Tie in the ends, secure and trim. Finish off the tie, then apply some cement (Fig. 7).

8

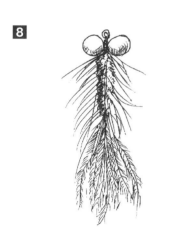

Your finished fly should look like the one in Fig. 8 when viewed from above.

BUCKTAIL STREAMER

MATERIALS

Sproat or limerick hook 2x long, size 4-10 (for saltwater fishing Mustad 34007 hook, size 5/0-/10)
Whisks (barbs) of cock hackle, dyed scarlet

Silver flat tinsel
Bucktail, natural brown and white or dyed

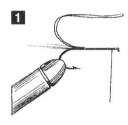

Start off by whipping the hook with thread and then tying in a few whisks of scarlet cock hackle. Tie in the flat tinsel (Fig. 1).

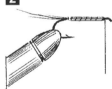

Wind the tinsel along the shank of the hook to near the head. Secure with a few turns of the thread and trim (Fig. 2).

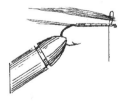

Take a small bunch of hair from a bucktail. White underneath with some brown strands on top is a popular way to tie this fly. Hold the bucktail along the top of the shank and **secure in place with a few firm but not tight turns** of the thread (Fig. 3).

Trim the ends if necessary, but if you have cut the bucktail at the right place and sat it correctly on top of the hook you should not have to trim it.

4

When you are satisfied that it looks right put a drop of cement on the head and let it soak in. Now tie a few short whisks of scarlet-dyed hackle under the chin. Trim the ends and then finish off the head (Fig. 4).

This pattern can be enhanced with the addition of eyes painted on the head. It can also be tied in a variety of colours.

If smelt are common in the estuarine and lower reaches of the river it can be tied with a gold tinsel body and a brown wing. Other variations use a combination of natural white and dyed bucktail. Green and white and blue and white are other popular colour combinations.

Tied on a stainless steel hook and in the larger sizes this is an excellent fly for catching saltwater species.

BURGLAR

MATERIALS

Limerick or sproat hook, size 2-8
Rabbit fur, dyed or natural

Cock neck hackles, black, honey
grizzle or brown

This lure, designed by George Gatchell, is an excellent copy of a cockabully. It's fairly simple to make as long as you take care, when building up the body, to make sure that the fur is distributed evenly around the hook. Otherwise you may take it out of the vice and find that the side away from you is uneven and looks a bit ratty. It is a good idea to use a small mirror to check the far side during tying.

This lure can be tied in black, brown or brindle. Since male cockabullies turn black during the mating season that's a good colour choice. Most cockabullies, though, are mottled. To imitate these I like to use well-marked honey grizzle cock neck hackles for the tail and a well-grizzled winter pelt from an old buck rabbit. The long, grey and brown mottled fur is peppered with long black guard hairs. Let's make one.

1

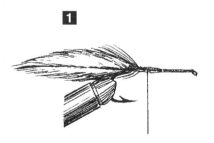

We have our hook in the vice, the thread has been wound on and four nicely marked cock neck hackles are matched and trimmed. Tie the first two in back to back and the next two up against the first pair. Tie in securely and cement (Fig. 1).

2

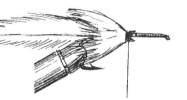

Take a snip of rabbit fur from the top of the pelt, cutting it close to the skin. Place it on top of the hook and make a couple of loose turns with the thread. This holds the fur in place as it is pushed and twisted around the shank to spread it evenly like a skirt. This can be accomplished by rolling the end of the fur between the thumb and forefinger of the left hand. **When it is in place, secure it with tight turns of the thread** (Fig. 2).

3

Check it with a mirror. If there is a gap on the far side, tie in another pinch of fur to fill it. Keep tying in pinches of fur, spreading it around the hook shank and securing it as you go. An occasional light dab of cement doesn't go amiss, but if the thread turns are pulled tight enough it shouldn't come to pieces during use. When the body is nearly full, tie in a neck hackle (Fig. 3).

Seize the end of the hackle in the pliers and wind it on in front of the fur, securing it with a couple of turns of thread. The hackle is then pulled back so that it slopes over the fur. Wind the thread around to keep it in place and then finish the head and paint it (Fig. 4).

This is a good night fly and is especially effective for fooling cagey old brownies. Know a hole in the river where a big brown lurks? Tie this pattern up and go after him long after it has turned dark.

DOLL FLY

MATERIALS

Limerick or sproat hook 3x long,
   size 6 or 8
4-ply acrylic knitting yarn, white,
   grey, green or brown

Hackle, dyed scarlet
Thread, the same colour as the
   back of the fly

The Doll Fly is a British pattern, and there it is tied on standard-length hooks, making it look fat and dumpy. When a long-shanked hook is used it looks racy, very much like a small smelt or whitebait.

The favourite dressing is a white body and grey back but it can be made up in any colour combination: grey and white, green and white, and brown and white are favoured recipes.

Start by preparing the acrylic yarn, which is bought by the ball. Cut off one length of each colour, about 100mm long. You will note that it is made up of four strands of yarn twisted together. Separate the strands and pull them tight between your fingers to take some of the twist out. Then take two strands and turn one of them over, reversing it and laying it along the other strand. Pull them tight again, running the yarn through your fingers. This way you will get nice even build-up of the body without any lumps or twists in the yarn.

1

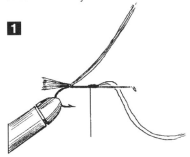

Take the length (2 strands) being used for the back of the fly and tie it in, just ahead of the bend of the hook. Now wind the thread along the hook and tie in the white body yarn (Fig. 1).

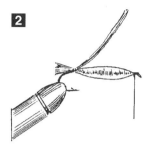

Wipe a bit of cement along the hook shank, then start building the white body. This may take a bit of practice. Wind toward the head first, then back over itself along the body to where the topping is tied in, then with careful turns go back again toward the head. You should find that the acrylic yarn lies flat and builds up a nice fish body shape. At this stage it should look like the one in Fig. 2.

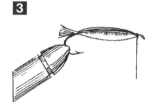

Now pull the back strip over, pulling it tight, and secure it at the head with several tight turns. Clip off the excess (Fig. 3).

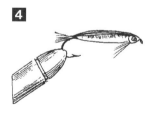

Pinch out a small tuft of scarlet hackles and tie them in short, at the throat, just under the head. Trim the ends off, then build up the head and finish it off (Fig. 4). If a grey back has been used in conjunction with grey tying thread, a couple of coatings of clear cement will give you a head that harmonises with the whole pattern. Paint on the eyes, yellow with a black centre, and the little lure will come to life.

Some tie this pattern with a body of luminous plastic strip which, when it is charged with a flashlight, glows in the dark.

GLO-BUG

MATERIALS

Sproat bend short-shanked hook,
   size 10-14

Glo-bug yarn
Heavy thread

Glo-bug or egg yarn comes in strands known as 'ropes'. You will need a heavy thread to tie the bug, preferably the same colour as the yarn. You will also need a heavy pair of shears or scissors to cut and trim the yarn – the little scissors used for normal tying just aren't up to the job. It's time to raid the sewing box for some solid cutters.

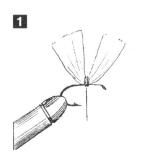

Take two sections of rope, each about 40mm long, and lay them one on top of the other. These can be differing shades of orange or red if a bi-coloured result is required. Start off by whipping the middle section of the hook shank with the tying thread, then put on a drop of cement. Some professionals use a little touch of superglue. If you try this, be careful not to get any on your fingers. Lay the strands along the top of the hook and secure with several tight turns (Fig. 1).

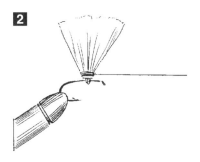

Now change direction and make several very tight turns around the butt of the strands (Fig. 2).

Next take the thread around the shank of the hook, just behind the eye, and finish it off. Grasp the upright yarn between the fingers, give it a twist, then shear it off (Fig. 3).

Take the bug from the vice, turn it over and cement the tying thread. When this is dry, fluff the yarn up with your fingers and it will splay out like a pompom (Fig. 4).

To make a **Muppet**, tie in chain bead or chromed lead eyes before the yarn is put in place.

KEITH'S KRAWLIE

MATERIALS

Limerick or sproat hook, size 2-4
Black hackles
Length of heavy nylon, 100g size
   (for eyes)
Grouse tail feather or similar

Big brown or olive hackle
Copper wire
Brown turkey tail
Olive chenille

Strip all the barbs off two black hackles and so that you are left with just the spines. These are your feelers.

To make the eyes burn the end of the short length of heavy nylon with a cigarette lighter. It will melt and produce small globules. You will need two.

The grouse tail feather cut and trimmed as in Fig. 4 makes the nippers.

You are now ready to put together this ugly but effective crayfish fly.

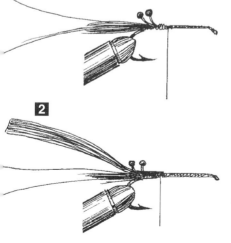

1

Start off by wrapping the hook shank with thread. Tie in a short bunch of brown turkey, then the feelers. When they have been secured, tie in the eyes and turn them up. Apply cement (Fig. 1).

2

Now tie in a long strip of turkey tail (Fig. 2).

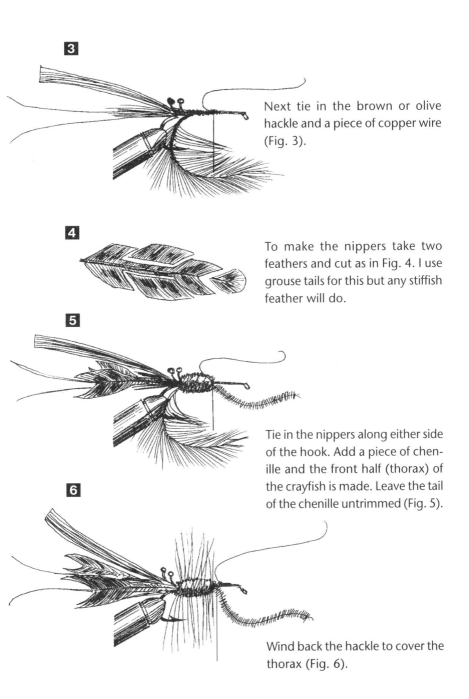

3

Next tie in the brown or olive hackle and a piece of copper wire (Fig. 3).

4

To make the nippers take two feathers and cut as in Fig. 4. I use grouse tails for this but any stiffish feather will do.

5

Tie in the nippers along either side of the hook. Add a piece of chenille and the front half (thorax) of the crayfish is made. Leave the tail of the chenille untrimmed (Fig. 5).

6

Wind back the hackle to cover the thorax (Fig. 6).

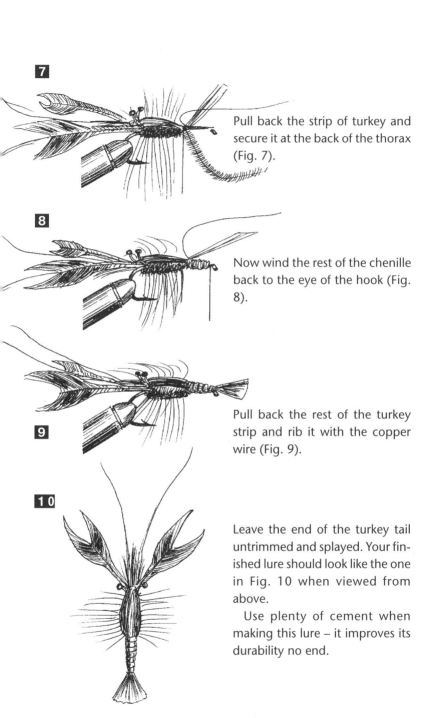

7

Pull back the strip of turkey and secure it at the back of the thorax (Fig. 7).

8

Now wind the rest of the chenille back to the eye of the hook (Fig. 8).

9

Pull back the rest of the turkey strip and rib it with the copper wire (Fig. 9).

10

Leave the end of the turkey tail untrimmed and splayed. Your finished lure should look like the one in Fig. 10 when viewed from above.

Use plenty of cement when making this lure – it improves its durability no end.

KILLER-TYPE FLIES

There are four popular killer-type fly patterns.

Mrs Simpson

MATERIALS

Limerick or sproat hook, size 4-8
Black squirrel tail
Wool or yarn, colour as required

Green/bronze rump feathers from
a cock pheasant

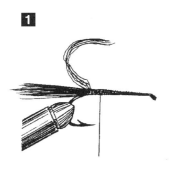

Tie in a tuft of black squirrel tail and a piece of body yarn (Fig. 1). 'A tuft' is not too big –remember you are not making a shaving brush, but at the same time it should not be wispy like a mandarin's moustache. Tie in a tuft and if it looks a bit miserable then add a bit more until it looks right. Have a look at patterns in the fly-shop trays. That'll give you a guide.

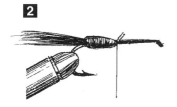

Make the rear half of the body and tie it off (Fig. 2).

3

Tie one cock pheasant rump feather in on either side. This can be tricky: **the secret is to hold them in place with moderately firm turns**. Then adjust the two feathers so that the spines are level with the body. When you are happy that they are straight and not cocked out at an angle, **make several tight turns to secure them** (Fig. 3).

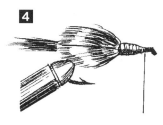

4

Take another piece of body yarn, tie it in and form the front section of the body. Start off by winding it back over the base of the two side feathers, then forward toward the head. Tie off, leaving room to finish the head (Fig. 4).

5

Take four more feathers. We are going to tie in two on each side. Start with one on each side. Remember to use light turns of the thread to hold them in place, then make certain that they are lying flat and straight against the sides. When you are happy, place another feather on top further along and go through the same process. When everything is nice and straight, finish off the fly with tight turns of the thread. Don't wind these tight turns too far back or the side feathers will splay out and twist. They should lie nicely alongside the fly (Fig. 5).

Hamill's Killer

MATERIALS

Limerick or sproat hook, sizes 4-8
Black squirrel tail
Golden pheasant tippets
Wool or yarn, green, yellow or red

Grey partridge plumage (or small grey mallard flanks), dyed olive green

This fly is tied exactly the same way as the Mrs Simpson except that a small bunch of golden pheasant tippets is laid over the top of the tail (Fig. 6).

The sides are of partridge plumage or mallard flanks instead of cock pheasant rump feathers.

Leslie's Lure

MATERIALS

Limerick or sproat hook, size 4-8
Grey speckled turkey secondary
   quill or a bunch of fibres from a
   cock pheasant tail

Wool or yarn, colour as required
Wing coverlets or small neck
   plumage from a hen pheasant

This fly has a tail of rolled speckled turkey or a bunch of fibres from a cock pheasant tail (Fig. 7).

Apart from that it is tied exactly the same as the previous two patterns. For some reason, this is the easiest of all the killer patterns to tie. The small hen pheasant feathers are sympathetic and lie nicely alongside the fly.

Lord's Killer

MATERIALS

Limerick or sproat hook, size 4-8
Black squirrel tail
Wool or yarn, colour as required

Body plumage from a woodcock
(up to 10 on each side)

This pattern is a great fish-catcher but a swine to tie. In the larger sizes it needs to be tied with three or even four body segments, and where in the other patterns one or two feathers suffice for each tie-in, with the soft woodcock plumage it is always necessary to lay three or even four feathers on top of each other to get a nice full tie (Fig. 8).

But when you get it right, having used at least a dozen or maybe 20 feathers to fill up the sides, you will have a fly to be proud of. What a pity to have it chewed up by trout!

LUMINOUS FLIES

MATERIALS
Luminous strips, beads or paint
Fly pattern as you wish

On the darkest of nights a fly that glows can be deadly. Luminous materials are available from all fly-tying shops and may be incorporated in any fly pattern you wish.

I have shown a few examples here. They can be tied on all sizes of hooks, but as with regular patterns, if the fish are hard to catch on the night, a small version will often be more successful than a larger one.

Fig. 1 shows a Doll Fly tied with a body of lumo strip.

Next is a Craig's Night Time version with a glow body (Fig. 2).

A luminous bead has been used to form the head of the fly in Fig. 3.

Luminous paint has been added to the body of the night fly in Fig. 4.

Basically, it doesn't matter too much what pattern you use, as long as it glows. You can let your imagination run riot on this one!

MARABOU STREAMER

MATERIALS

Limerick or sproat hook, size 2-8   Olive chenille
Black marabou plumes   Black cock neck hackle

The marabou is a popular fly. In the black versions it is highly thought of as a night fly, while the olive and brightly coloured ones are good for day use. The gaudy ones–bright oranges and pinks– are used for catching winter-run rainbows.

A popular night version has a body of olive chenille with black marabou tail and wings. Let's tie it.

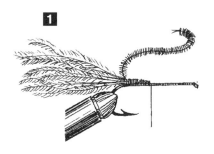

Secure the hook in the vice and whip it with thread. Trim and tie in a bunch of soft black marabou fibres from a plume. Tie in a short piece of olive chenille and apply a drop of cement, allowing it to soak in (Fig. 1).

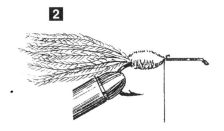

Since the body of this fly is to be in two pieces, wind the chenille to halfway along the shank, then tie it in and trim it (Fig. 2).

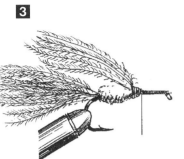

3

Now a wing of black marabou is tied in and secured (Fig. 3).

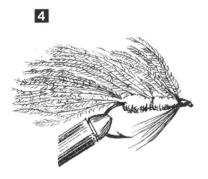

Tie in and wind around another piece of chenille and the front half of the body is finished. Add another wing of marabou and, if you like, a black hackle wound around (Fig. 4).

The hackle gives the fly a little more bulk, which some anglers prefer, but others don't bother.

Either way it is a good pattern and, in its many colour variations, it can be used right around the clock.

RABBIT FLY

MATERIALS

Limerick or sproat hook, sizes 2-8
Cock hackles, dyed and natural
Chenille, colour as required

Oval tinsel
Strips of rabbit pelt

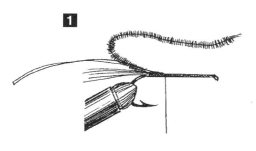

Set the hook in the vice, wind the thread along the shank and tie in a small bunch of dyed cock hackle whisks. These should be red if the body is to be yellow or orange, yellow if the body is to be green or red. Next tie in the strip of tinsel and the end of the chenille (Fig. 1).

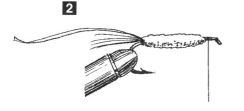

Wind on the chenille, forming the body (Fig. 2).

Before tying in the strip of rabbit fur we have to prepare it. I prefer that the pelt be stretched and tacked when green. When it is dried, you may need the help of an engineer's vice.

underside of pelt

Put the neck end into the jaws, then holding it taut, cut out strips using a hobby or lino knife. A scalpel will do if the skin is thin but the hobby knife will make a better job.

Be careful making these downward cuts if you want to end up with usable strips. They need to be about 3mm wide. Trim to shape, taking great care to cut just the skin and not the fur (Fig. 3).

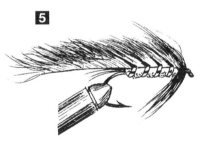

Lay the strip along the top of the body and secure it at the head with several turns of the tying thread. Take the tinsel with the pliers and, lifting the fur of the rabbit strip with a dubbing needle (as with a Matuku style fly,pp68-69), run it in nice even turns to secure the strip (Fig. 4).

A hackle is not necessary for this style of fly but if you like you can tie one in and wind it on (Fig. 5).
    The rule is to use a hackle that harmonises with the colour pattern. A honey grizzle or brown one goes well with orange or yellow bodies, and a dark furnace with green or red. Some tiers like to use a hackle the same colour as the body. The choice is yours, and you can tie it the way you want it to look. Don't forget an all-black Rabbit Fly – excellent for after dark.

If you don't wish to, or cannot get your own pelt, you can buy strips of tanned pelt but the soft, supple skin is difficult to trim to shape.

MATUKU-STYLE FLIES

Matuku-style flies are very popular, both for flycasting and for trolling. It always pays to have a selection of them in your flybox.

This style of tie is used for many patterns. While the materials may differ and the end result appear totally different from pattern to pattern, they all have one thing in common: their shape and the manner in which they are constructed. The following are some of the more popular patterns that are tied this way.

Parson's Glory

MATERIALS

Limerick or sproat hook, size 2-8
Scarlet hackle whisks

Yellow chenille
Gold oval tinsel

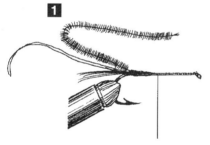

Honey grizzle cock neck hackle
Let's start. The hook is in the vice, the tag of scarlet whisks has been tied, followed by the strip of tinsel and the end of the piece of yellow chenille (Fig. 1).

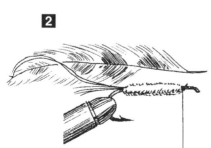

Wind on the chenille to form the body, leaving that vital space behind the eye that we will need for finishing the head. Take four carefully selected hackles and place two of them back to back. Lay the other two hackles along the outsides, ensuring that the tips are even. Pull off a section of the fluff and lower filaments of the feathers (Fig. 2).

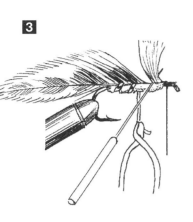

3

Lay on the wing hackles and hold them in place with several tight turns of the thread. Snip off the butt ends. Take the end of the tinsel in the pliers and wind it through the feathers, opening the feather with the point of a bodkin (Fig. 3).

The tinsel should be wound on in nice even turns. Use a piece no longer than 40-50mm or you will have trouble with the pliers hitting the table as you wind it around.

4

Wind the thread around to secure the last turn of the tinsel, which is then snipped off (Fig. 4).

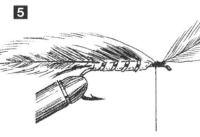

5

Now tie in a hackle that has had the ends trimmed (Fig. 5).

6

Wind the hackle on, pull it back and secure with several turns of the thread. When the fly is complete, finish off the head and paint it (Fig. 6).

Hart's Creek

MATERIALS

Limerick or sproat hook, size 2-8
Tag of scarlet hackle whisks
Body of black chenille

Ribbing of silver oval tinsel
Wing and hackle of black cock
  neck hackle

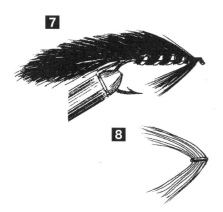

This fly (Fig. 7) is tied exactly as a Parson's Glory except that a chin hackle is used instead of a full wound one. You cut a small snippet of hackle from a feather (Fig. 8), hold it under the chin of the fly and tie it in. This style of hackle is ideal if a slim, lightly dressed fly is needed, such as a small Grey Ghost.

Albino

MATERIALS

Limerick or sproat hook, size 4-8
Tag of scarlet hackle whisks
Body of white chenille or wool

Ribbing of silver oval tinsel
Wing and hackle of white cock
  neck hackle

Grey Ghost

MATERIALS

Limerick or sproat hook, size 4-10
Tag of scarlet hackle whisks
Body of silver flat tinsel

Ribbing of silver oval tinsel
Wing and hackle of dyed grey
  cock neck hackles

Jack's Sprat

As for Grey Ghost except that badger hackles are used instead of dyed grey.

Taupo Tiger

As for Parson's Glory except that badger hackles are used instead of honey grizzle. Another distinguishing feature of this pattern is its head, which is always painted red.

Yellow Lady

As for Taupo Tiger except yellow dyed hackles are used. This fly also has a red head.

All of these Matuku-style patterns may be enhanced by painting eyes on the head.

MUDDLER MINNOW

MATERIALS

Speckled secondary feathers from a turkey's wing

Gold flat tinsel

Piece of pelt from a white tail deer

The Muddler Minnow is a good pattern to learn to accomplish the art of spinning deer hair (see Basic Techniques). These days we have many patterns derived from the Muddler, as well as dry flies that use bodies made from spun and clipped deer hair. Once mastered the technique is not difficult.

We will tie a Muddler first, then look at some derivations of that pattern.

If you can't get white tail hair then fallow deer is a good second choice. Sika deer hair is okay in parts; search around a hide if you come across one. You are looking for round hairs, not flat ones. Except for around the rump, red deer hair is too flat and hard. I have used roe deer pelt and that was fine. Your local fly-tying shop will help you.

First tie in a piece of speckled turkey feather for the tail. This should be rolled, the same way you would roll a piece of feather when winging a wet fly (see March Brown Wet Fly). Then tie in the tinsel (Fig. 1).

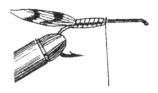

Wind on the gold tinsel body (Fig. 2).

3

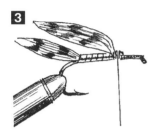

Now tie in the rolled wing of speckled turkey Fig. 3).

4

We now have the front third of the hook free. Spin on a deer-hair head (see Basic Techniques). Fig. 4 shows the finished result.

Matuku Muddler

5

This is a Matuku-style fly with a clipped deer head (Fig. 5).

Rabbit Muddler

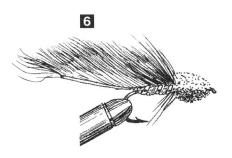

Take a Rabbit Fly and give it a Muddler head (Fig. 6).

Marabou Muddler

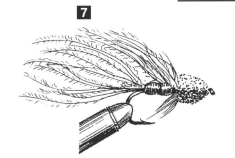

A Marabou pattern can also be combined in this way (Fig. 7).

Deer-hair Mouse

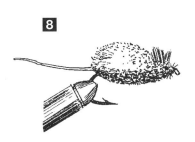

This fly is tied using the same principle. Tie in a piece of bootlace or string for a tail, then build up the body. The ears and whiskers are shaped with a bit of careful sculpturing using the points of your scissors (Fig. 8).

You know that old story about how those big cannibal browns just can't resist a swimming mouse? Here's your chance to test it!

RED SETTER, FUZZY WUZZY, DAPPLED DOG

These three patterns are tied using exactly the same processes. All that differs are the materials used.

Red Setter

MATERIALS

Limerick or sproat hook, size 2-8
Brown squirrel tail
Orange chenille

Cock neck hackle, natural red or
   ginger

Fuzzy Wuzzy

MATERIALS

Limerick or sproat hook, size 2-8
Black squirrel tail

Chenille, red, black, green or orange
Cock neck hackles, dyed black

Dappled Dog

MATERIALS

Limerick or sproat hook, size 2-8
Grey squirrel tail
Grizzle cock neck hackles

Chenille, fluorescent orange, pink
   or lime

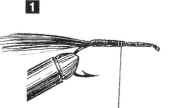

Clamp the hook in the vice, wind the thread along the shank and give it a light coat of cement. Tie in a small bunch of hair from the squirrel tail. Cut the butts at an angle, not square. This way, when the thread has been wound along the tail to secure it to the hook, you will get a nice taper, not a sudden step down (Fig. 1).

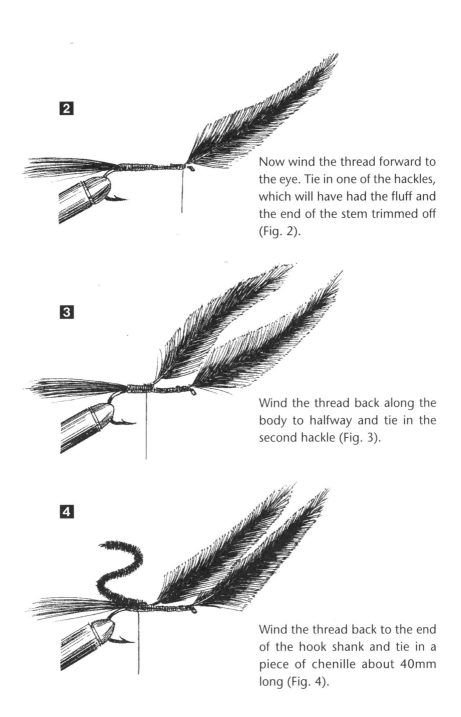

2

Now wind the thread forward to the eye. Tie in one of the hackles, which will have had the fluff and the end of the stem trimmed off (Fig. 2).

3

Wind the thread back along the body to halfway and tie in the second hackle (Fig. 3).

4

Wind the thread back to the end of the hook shank and tie in a piece of chenille about 40mm long (Fig. 4).

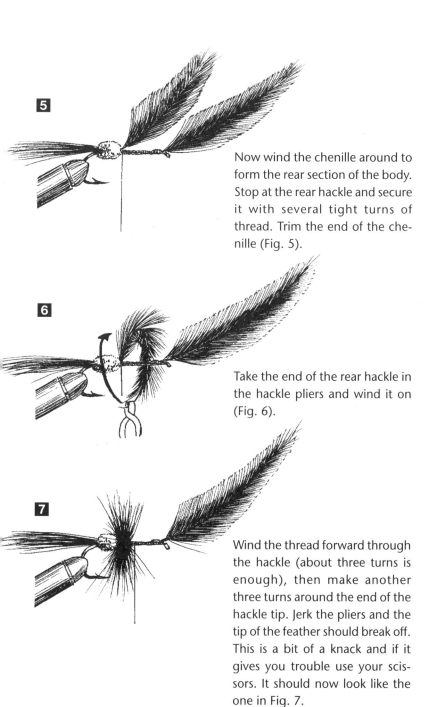

5

Now wind the chenille around to form the rear section of the body. Stop at the rear hackle and secure it with several tight turns of thread. Trim the end of the chenille (Fig. 5).

6

Take the end of the rear hackle in the hackle pliers and wind it on (Fig. 6).

7

Wind the thread forward through the hackle (about three turns is enough), then make another three turns around the end of the hackle tip. Jerk the pliers and the tip of the feather should break off. This is a bit of a knack and if it gives you trouble use your scissors. It should now look like the one in Fig. 7.

8

Pull the hackle points back and secure them in that position by making several turns of the thread over the bases (Fig. 8).

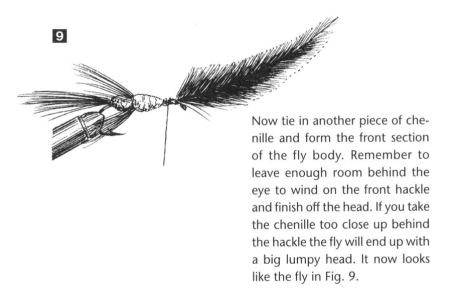

9

Now tie in another piece of chenille and form the front section of the fly body. Remember to leave enough room behind the eye to wind on the front hackle and finish off the head. If you take the chenille too close up behind the hackle the fly will end up with a big lumpy head. It now looks like the fly in Fig. 9.

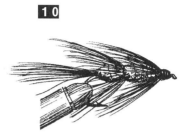

Wind on the front hackle exactly the same way as you did the back one, except that while the rear hackle was wound forwards, the front one is wound back. Secure and trim the end of the feather.

Pull the hackles back, secure in place with several turns of the thread, assure yourself that everything looks good, then finish off the head (Fig. 10).

Apply a couple of coats of head paint and you should have a fly to be proud of.

This style of tie is a great one for learning how to manage hackles and will stand you in good stead when hackling smaller fly patterns later on. These three patterns are very popular river and lake flies. Tied in their many variations, and in different sizes, they will provide you with patterns for using both day and night.

SMELT FLIES

All five styles of smelt fly illustrated here are good fish-catching patterns and are simple to tie.

Olive Smelt

MATERIALS

Limerick or sproat hook, size 6-10
Cock neck hackles, dyed olive

Olive wool yarn or floss
Gold flat tinsel

This is a simple fly for those who have trouble tying on the wings in the normal Matuku style.

First tie in two slim olive feathers in back to back to form the tail. The gold tinsel enhances the olive body, imparting a flash. For the neck hackle it pays to use one a bit on the long side. Sweep it back and secure it so that it veils the body (Fig. 1).

Mallard Smelt

MATERIALS

Limerick or sproat hook, size 6-10
Silver speckled mallard flank feather
Wool or yarn, colour as required

Silver or gold flat tinsel
Pale grey hackle

This small pattern (Fig. 2) is a top fly. The tail is made by cutting a narrow snip from the mallard flank then doubling it over before tying it in.

Hawk and Rabbit

MATERIALS

Limerick or sproat hook, size 6-10
White primary feather from a swan
  or goose

Wool or yarn, colour as required
Pinch of rabbit fur

The original of this fly used a slip of feather taken from the pale primary of a harrier hawk, but this is now a protected bird.

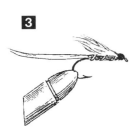

The tail is put in exactly the same way as that of the Mallard Smelt. The slim body is made and ribbed with tinsel, then you tie in the small tuft of rabbit fur above the body.

Some seeing this fly (Fig. 3) for the first time think it an unlikely fly but there are others who know better.

Grey Ghost (Fig. 4) and **Jack's Sprat** are two other styles of smelt fly, described in the Matuku fly section. As smelt patterns I believe they perform best on smaller hooks.

For a slender fly use only two hackles back to back to form the wing instead of the four recommended in the heavier patterns.

WOOLLY BUGGER

MATERIALS

Limerick or sproat hook, size 2-8
Marabou, dyed olive
Olive chenille

Gold oval tinsel
Grizzle hackle, dyed olive

This is a top fly that will prove just as effective after dark as it is during daylight. It can also be tied brown or black.

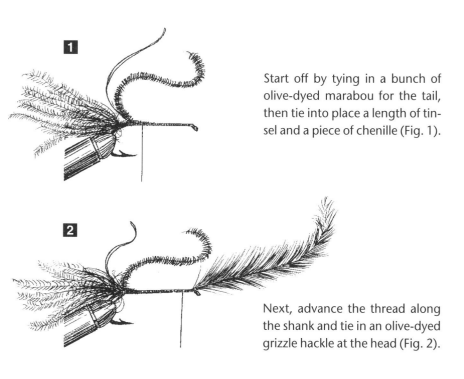

1

Start off by tying in a bunch of olive-dyed marabou for the tail, then tie into place a length of tinsel and a piece of chenille (Fig. 1).

2

Next, advance the thread along the shank and tie in an olive-dyed grizzle hackle at the head (Fig. 2).

3

Wind on the chenille to form the body (Fig. 3).

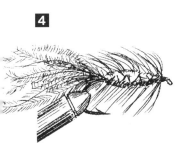

4

To finish the fly use the hackle pliers to wind the hackle back along the body toward the tail using open turns. Then, taking another set of hackle pliers, grip the end of the tinsel and wind it back through the feather to the head (Fig. 4).

Be sure to counter-rotate the tinsel to ensure that the stem of the hackle feather is properly secured.

MARCH BROWN WET FLY

MATERIALS

Limerick or sproat hook, size 10-14   Hare fur
Brown partridge hackles   Hen pheasant secondary wing
Fine gold wire   feather

The old style of wet fly is not used much these days but it is a very useful pattern. One of these flies on a floating line in the dusk when the caddis flies are starting to hatch can be a deadly way to fish.

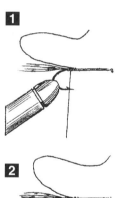

Start off by whipping the hook shank, tying in a few whisks of partridge hackle to form the tail and then a length of fine gold wire for the ribbing (Fig. 1).

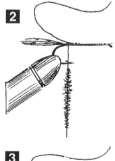

Next take a **pinch** of hare fur and spin it onto the tying thread (Fig. 2).

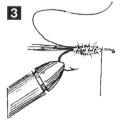

Form the body by winding the dubbed fur onto the hook shank (Fig. 3).

Wind on the wire ribbing in nice even turns to secure the body (Fig. 4).

5

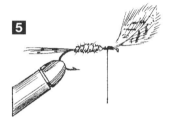

Tie in a partridge hackle (Fig. 5).

6

Wind the hackle on, pull the ends under and secure it in position with a couple of turns of the thread (Fig. 6).

7

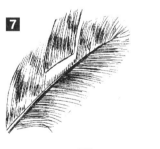

We must now prepare the wing. Take a secondary quill from a hen pheasant wing and cut out a short section (Fig. 7).

8

Roll the piece of feather as shown in Fig. 8.

Take this winging material in the fingers of the left hand, place it over the head of the fly and tie it on (Fig. 9).

This is a tricky manoeuvre: it is an up and down motion, not a circular one. If you wind the thread round and round you will twist the wing down the far side of the hook where it will probably split into an untidy bundle. By taking the thread up and then down, you will pull the piece of winging material down in a straight line, compressing the butts one on top of the other so that the wing sits nicely on top. This is the secret of winging wet flies.

When you have it in place, snip off the ends, finish off the head and cement (Fig. 10)!

Be careful with these heads – they have to be small. Remember that two tight, careful turns are better than 20 loose, sloppy ones.

You will use exactly the same tie for making other wet flies: all that differ are the materials used. Some other wet fly patterns you might like to tie using this method (together with the ingredients required) follow on the next page.

Red Spinner

Materials
Tail whisks: Barbs from a natural red cock feather
Body: Red floss silk with a gold tinsel rib
Wings: Mallard primary wing feather
Hackle: Natural red cock or hen

Red-tipper Governor

Materials
Tag or tip: Red floss silk
Body: Bronze peacock herl
Wing: Secondary quill feather from a hen pheasant
Hackle: Natural red cock or hen

Twilight Beauty

Materials
Tail whisks: Barbs from a ginger cock hackle
Body: Black floss silk
Wing: Primary feather from a blackbird or native grey duck wing
Hackle: Ginger cock or hen hackle

You will note that for the hackles either cock or hen may be used, but if the former is chosen it should be short in the barb and soft. Stiff hackles are better used in making dry flies.

WAYS TO WEIGHT A NYMPH BODY

There are several ways of weighting a nymph to make it sink. We all know that unless the trout are feeding off the surface they are down on the bottom of the pool, and a fly drifted in front of their noses has a much better chance of being taken than one drifting along well above their heads.

Copper wire is an easy method and any fly tier should have several spools of it in various gauges. It is wound on to form a shape that suggests the form of an insect. This forms the underbody and the materials for making the abdomen and thorax are dressed over the top of the wire.

In shallower streams you do not need really heavy patterns. A bit of experimentation will tell you exactly how much wire you need to sink the fly to the required depth.

Lead wire is very effective for getting flies down deep in large, fast rivers. It is pliable and easily wound on. It pays to have several spools of varying gauges to suit the size of the hook being used.

3

Chain bead eyes start off as a length of bath tap bead chain from a plumbing supplier. Using side cutters, turn it into pairs of eyes. In really fast, deep waters these metal bead eyes are sometimes combined with a leaded body to make a super-heavy pattern. You might use one of these on the Tongariro River when fishing for winter-run rainbows.

4

Purpose-made lead chromed eyes are super-efficient, but on windy days these extra-heavy flies are a menace. Anyone who has been hit on the back of the head by one will know exactly what I am talking about.

Combined with lead in the body, these flies, often referred to as bombs, are sometimes used purely as sinkers. They are combined with a number 14 pattern tied onto a dropper and this will be the effective hooking fly. The use of sinkers is prohibited but by using these legal but over-weighted patterns, anglers get to the bottom of the deepest holes. Both the bead chain eyes and the chromed lead ones are secured to the fly by using the figure-eight system of tying (Fig. 5).

5

CADDIS GRUB

MATERIALS

Limerick or sproat hook, size 10-14, or specialist caddis larva hook	Copper wire
	Floss or yarn, white, grey, brown or green
Lead wire	Strands of bronze peacock herl

This very deadly pattern is simplicity itself. Much of its success depends upon the lead underbody, which takes the fly down deep where it drifts above the bottom. That's where caddis-feeding trout are to be found.

Grey and green versions of this pattern are good fish-catching patterns but the brown and white ones are also successful. One technique of using them is on a sinking line with a very short (300mm) leader. Cast them up, across and let them drift and roll around in the current before retrieving them and making another cast.

Let's get tying.

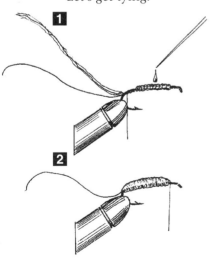

1

Place the hook in the vice, bind the shank with thread and then tie in a length of copper wire and a piece of yarn. Wind on some lead wire in close, even turns (Fig. 1). Cement.

2

Next, take the yarn and wind it around to form the body. Leave about 4mm of room at the head of the fly (Fig. 2).

3

Take the copper wire and rib the fly with regularly spaced turns. Secure and clip off the end of the wire. Now tie in two strands of peacock herl (Fig. 3).

4

Wind the herl on to fill in behind the head of the fly, secure it with several turns of thread and clip it off, leaving a couple of short butts sticking out. Tie off and cement the head (Fig. 4).

5

Specially made caddis hooks enable you to tie a fly with a curved body like the one in Fig. 5.

CREEPER

MATERIALS

Sproat hook 2x long, size 8-12
Brown chenille
Copper wire
Lead wire

Biots from duck, goose or turkey
   primary quills
Speckled brown turkey feather
Long soft brown cock hackle

This is a good pattern, especially on stony rocky streams and rivers – the ideal habitat for the creeper.

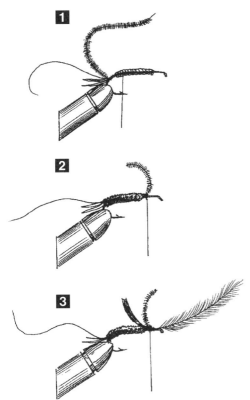

Wrap the shank with thread, then tie in two brown biots. These are the stiff barbs (often dyed) on the leading edge of a bird's primary quills. You can use quills from duck, goose or turkey (from fly-tying shops if you do not shoot). I like the ones from the wing quills of the paradise duck. They are dark and don't need dyeing.

Tie in a length of copper wire and a piece of chenille. Wrap a length of lead wire around the hook shank (Fig. 1).

Now wind the chenille along approximately two-thirds of the body. Do not trim the end (Fig. 2).

Tie in a slip of turkey feather and the long hackle (Fig. 3).

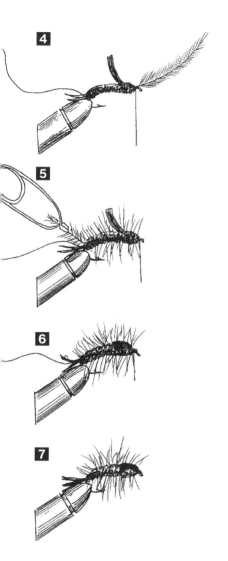

Wind the chenille forwards to form the thorax (Fig. 4).

Take the hackle with the pliers and wind it back to the end of the body (Fig. 5).

Now take the copper wire and rib the whole of the body to behind the eye of the hook (Fig. 6).

This serves two purposes: it will keep the hackle in place and also give the fly added weight.

Pull the turkey strip over, tie it in and trim. Finish off the head (Fig. 7).

Using the scissors, trim the whole hackle to leave short stubs (Fig. 8).

DAMSEL NYMPH

MATERIALS

Sproat hook 3x long, size 10-14
Copper wire
Marabou plume, dyed olive

Olive chenille
Hen hackle, dyed olive

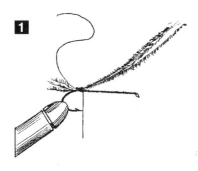

Wrap the hook with thread, tie in a length of fine copper wire and select three strands from an olive-dyed marabou plume. Tie in the tips (Fig. 1).

Wind the marabou two-thirds of the way along the hook shank and secure it with the thread. Wind on the copper wire to form a ribbing and secure the marabou. Tie in a short piece of olive chenille and then the olive hackle at the head (Fig. 2).

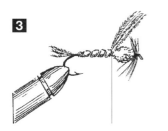

Next, wind on the chenille to form the thorax. Secure and trim it. Wind on and secure the hackle (Fig. 3).

4

Pull the butt ends of the marabou forward to form the wing cases. Tie them in, trim them and finish the head (Fig. 4). Cement.

This pattern can also be followed using wrapped wool or dubbed fur in place of the marabou. There are several variations and it can be tied in a variety of colours, but in my book olive is by far the most successful.

DRAGONFLY NYMPH OR MUDEYE

MATERIALS

Sproat hook 2x long, size 6-12
Mallard flank feather, dyed olive
Olive chenille
Soft hen hackle, dyed olive

Small wing coverlet from hen
  pheasant or duck wing
Piece of heavy nylon monofilament (for eyes)

Tie in a tuft of barbs from the base of the mallard flank feather. Now tie in the end of the chenille (Fig. 1).

Wind the chenille along the hook to form the abdomen (Fig. 2).

Take the small coverlet feather and nip out the top of it (Fig. 3).

Tie this piece in on top of the hook so that it sits over the front half of the abdomen. Then tie in a piece of feather snipped from the mallard flank. Now tie in the soft olive hackle at the head (Fig. 4).

5

Wind the chenille along to form the thorax. Wind in the hackle and secure with the thread, then pull the slip of mallard flank over to form the wing cases. Secure them with the thread and trim (Fig. 5).

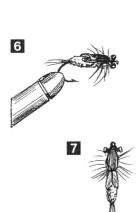

6

Burn the ends of the nylon mono-filament to make two eyes. When they have hardened tie them into the head of the fly, securing them with a figure of eight. Finish off the head and cement (Fig. 6).

7

Viewed from above, the finished fly should look like the one in Fig. 7.

Deer-hair Variation

A variation of this pattern is tied with a head of clipped deer hair. This pattern is ideal for fishing just under the surface. It suggests a nymph that has left the bottom and is looking for a rock or reed on which to climb out of the water, preparatory to hatching.

8

First you tie in the whisks and make the abdomen (Fig. 8).

Tie in the wing cases (Fig. 9).

Spin on a head of deer hair (see Basic Techniques), clip it to shape and hitch the thread to secure the finish. The finished product should look like the one in Fig. 10.

You can also tie a brown version of this pattern. Tie it in several sizes: trout feed just as avidly on immature nymphs as they do on full-grown ones.

EMERGER NYMPH

MATERIALS

Cock neck hackle

Dry fly hook, size 10-14

Hare fur

Small ball of polystyrene foam

Small square of nylon mesh
    snipped from a pair of tights

This pattern is made to float along the surface of the water. It is intended to represent a nymph in the process of emerging from its nymphal case as it drifts along the current. The small ball of polystyrene keeps the pattern suspended on the surface.

First make the abdomen of the fly. This is done by wrapping the hook with thread, leaving the tail of it loose to be used for securing and ribbing the body.

Tie in a few whisks of cock neck hackle to represent the tail, and make an abdomen of dubbed hare fur which is wound on and then ribbed with the tail of the tying thread (Fig. 1).

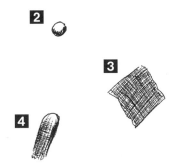

The little ball of polystyrene can be bought from a hobby shop or filched from a bean bag (Fig. 2). Place the ball in the square of nylon mesh (Fig. 3) and pull the edges of the mesh together (Fig. 4).

5

Secure this float on top of the fly (Fig. 5). Be careful with cement at this stage as the solvent in the cement may dissolve the plastic ball if it touches it.

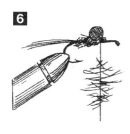

6

Take a pinch of hare fur with a lot of long straggly guard hairs in it and dub (twist) it onto the thread (Fig. 6).

7

Wind the dubbed thread onto the front of the hook, secure the thread, trim it and cement the head carefully (Fig. 7).

This is a good pattern that can be tied in several colours, using reddish brown, black or blue dun dubbing furs.

GOLD BEAD NYMPH

Here are two popular nymph patterns that have been adapted to have a brass bead incorporated in their dressing.

These beads are available from all fly-tying shops and they make for a very successful fish-catching nymph pattern. The bright gold bead not only seems to help attract trout but it also gives the fly added weight, an essential element of most successful nymphing patterns.

You slip the bead on over the shank of the hook before making up the fly. Wrap the tying thread on close behind the head to force it up against the eye of the hook. A drop of cement or superglue helps to keep it in place.

Theo's Brass Bead Hare and Copper Nymph

Theo's Brass Bead Pheasant Tail Nymph

HALFBACK NYMPH AND VARIANTS

MATERIALS

Sproat hook 2x long, size 10-14
Small soft hackle (cock or hen),
   natural red
Fine copper wire

Peacock herl
Turkey tail feather
Lead wire (optional)

The Halfback and its variations are top fish-catching patterns. In its smaller sizes it is an excellent representation of the mayfly nymph *Coloburiscus humeralsi*.

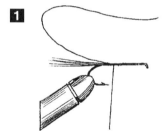

Wrap the hook with thread, then tie in some whisks of red cock neck hackle and a piece of fine copper wire (Fig. 1).

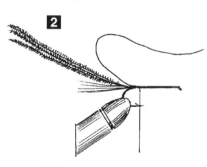

Next, tie in the ends of some strands of peacock herl (Fig. 2). For a larger hook several strands will be needed, whereas on the smaller sizes two or even one strand will do. If required, tie in the lead wire to weight the nymph at this stage also.

Wind on the herl to halfway along the shank, forming the abdomen. Then wind on the copper wire to help strengthen the brittle herl (Fig. 3).

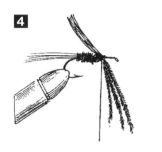

Tie in a snip of turkey tail to make the wing cases (Fig. 4).

Take the small soft hackle and tie it in at the head (Fig. 5).

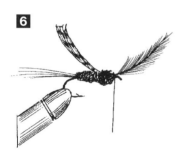

Wind on the rest of the herl to form the thorax, tie it in and trim (Fig. 6).

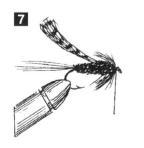

Wind on the hackle a couple of turns and secure with the thread (Fig. 7).

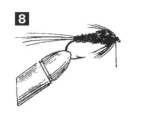

Pull over the piece of turkey tail to form the wing cases, tie it in, then trim. Finish the head and cement it (Fig. 8).

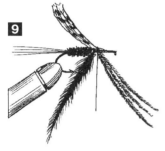

There is a variation to this tie. Instead of tying the hackle in at the head, you can secure it under the wing cases as shown in Fig. 9.

After the herl thorax is made the hackle is wound over it up to the head. The fly is then finished off in the normal way with a full palmer-like hackle right along the thorax (Fig. 10). (A palmer hackle is wound along the body in widely spaced turns.)

Another variation is the **Flashback**, which is a standard Halfback but with a wing case of silver tinsel (Fig. 11). This pattern is very popular on the Taupo rivers for fishing migratory rainbows.

Yet another variation is the **Bead-eyed Halfback**. In this case a pair of chain bead or chromed lead eyes give extra glitter to the pattern as well as serving to help it to sink more rapidly in fast water (Fig. 12).

HARE & COPPER NYMPH

MATERIALS

Limerick or sproat hook, size 10-16
Cock neck hackles, black and
    natural red
Copper or lead wire

Hare fur
Turkey or pheasant feather
    (optional)

This pattern has to be the most successful and popular nymph pattern ever. It is so versatile. It can be tied large and shaggy or small and neat. It can be clipped to suggest a caddis case or tied to resemble a hatching sedge pupa. It can be tied on a long-shanked hook, dressed slim and be used as a very successful imitation of a darting damsel nymph. It can be fished unweighted just under the surface or heavily weighted, rolling along among the rocks and stones of the stream bottom. Tied on a large hook and shaped appropriately it can be made to represent a small minnow.

All these ways of tying a Hare & Copper are based on the tie I am about to explain to you.

1

Start off by wrapping the hook with thread and tying in some dark whisks of cock hackle (Fig. 1).

2

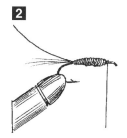

Tie in a length of copper wire and wrap it many turns around the hook to weight the fly. THe end is left protruding at the bend. This will be used to rib the fly. Use lead wire instead if a faster-sinking pattern is required (Fig. 2).

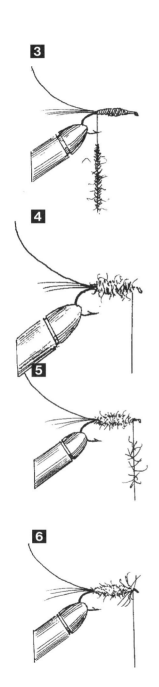

3

Take a small pinch of hare fur and spin it onto the tying thread. A little rub of cement along the thread will help the fur to stick if you have trouble spinning it on with your fingers (Fig. 3).

4

Wind the fur onto the hook (Fig. 4).

5

Take some long straggly guard furs from the hare pelt and twist them onto the thread (Fig. 5).

6

Wind these around the fly just behind the head (Fig. 6).

Wind on the wire rib, finish off, secure and cement the head (Fig. 7).

Some like to have a wing case of turkey or pheasant feather. This is tied in during the process and pulled over, secured and trimmed before the head is finished (Fig. 8).

MIDGE PUPA

MATERIALS

Sproat hook, size 12-18   Bronze peacock herl
Short tufts of white feather or floss   Grey tying thread
Body floss or yarn, red, green or black

Easy to tie, the Midge Pupa is a very effective stillwater pattern.

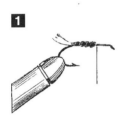

When you put the hook in the vice and wrap the thread, leave a tail of it hanging out and do not trim it off. You will use this to rib the abdomen of the fly.

Next, tie in a short length of white feather or floss to represent the tail filaments of the insect, then the body yarn. Red, green and black are favourite colours. Wind the yarn to halfway along the body, secure with the thread, then use the tail end of the thread to rib the body (Fig. 1).

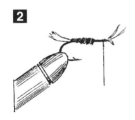

The next step is to tie in another set of white tufts at the head, to represent the filamentous antennae of the insect (Fig. 2).

Now tie in a couple of strands of bronze peacock herl (Fig. 3).

Wind them up to the eye of the hook, secure with the tying thread and snip off the ends. Finish off the head, trim off the thread and apply a drop of cement (Fig. 4).

I have illustrated this pattern with a straight body. Some prefer to tie it slightly around the bend of the hook. Take your pick. The trout seem to like it either way.

PHEASANT TAIL NYMPH

MATERIALS

Limerick or sproat hook, size 10-16
Fine copper wire
Bunch of fibres from a cock pheas-
    ant tail

Small hackle, natural red, furnace
    or black (optional)
Hare fur (optional)

This pattern should really be called Sawyer's Pheasant Tail, after the English water-keeper and angling authority who designed this extremely simple but deadly nymph pattern. Sawyer used no tying thread. He used the fine copper wire both for securing the components and building up the abdomen and thorax. Most of us use thread for the latter.

1

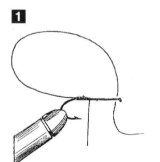

Wrap the hook with thread and whip in the end of the copper wire (Fig. 1). (If it's very fine it may pay to double it.)

2

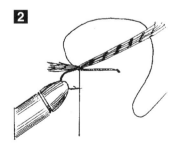

Now tie in the piece of pheasant tail (Fig. 2).

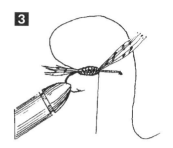

Advance the thread to halfway along the hook shank, then wind on the pheasant tail to form the abdomen. Secure with the thread (Fig. 3).

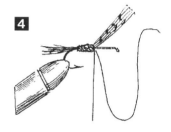

Wind the copper wire over the abdomen to serve as a ribbing (Fig. 4).

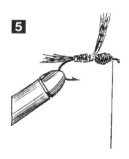

Now take the copper wire and with careful turns form the thorax (Fig. 5).

Pull the butts of the pheasant tail over the thorax to form the wing cases and tie in. Trim off ends, finish head and cement (Fig. 6).

Some like to add a hackle before forming the wing cases (Fig. 7), in which case your finished version will look like the one in Fig. 8.

Others like to spin a bit of fur dubbing onto the thread and wind it in over the thorax before pulling over and securing the wing cases. These are all variations on what is already a very successful pattern.

STONEFLY NYMPH

MATERIALS

Sproat hook 1x or 2x long, size 8-14   Mallard plumage, dyed olive
Goose biots, dyed olive   Lead wire for weighting if desired
Seal fur or substitute, dyed olive   Cock hackles
Gold ribbing wire

You will need to weight this fly if you are fishing deep rivers, but for smaller headwater streams tie them unweighted. A single split shot, squeezed on just above the tippet knot, can be used when necessary if fishing regulations permit it.

Start off by tying in two goose biots for the tail, then the gold ribbing. Spin a pinch of olive fur onto the tying thread (Fig. 1).

Form the abdomen by winding on the dubbed fur, then secure with several even turns of the ribbing wire (Fig. 2).

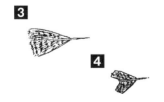

Take a mallard breast feather that has been dyed olive (Fig. 3) and trim it to shape to represent the emergent wings (Fig. 4).

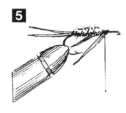

Tie in two more biots, one on either side just in front of the abdomen to represent legs (Fig. 5).

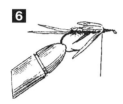

Tie in the mallard 'wings' (Fig. 6).

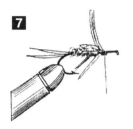

Tie in a slip of olive-dyed mallard plumage (Fig. 7).

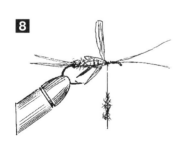

Strip the barbs off two cock hackles, trim the stems and tie the tips in to represent the antennae. Spin a pinch of olive fur onto the thread (Fig. 8).

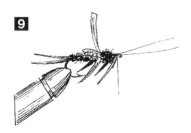

Bind on the fur to form the thorax, then tie in two more biots (Fig. 9).

1 0

Pull the slip of olive-dyed mallard plumage over the thorax, tie it in, trim and finish off the head (Fig. 10).

This pattern can be tied in either green or brown. Both are very effective, but the olive version is more popular.

WIGGLE-LEGGED NYMPH

MATERIALS

Limerick or sproat hook 2x long,
size 8-12
Olive chenille (2 shades)

Olive rubber legging material
(from fly-tying shops)
Goose wing, dyed olive

This system of tying can be applied to most nymph patterns. The one I have illustrated here is a version of the Green Stonefly nymph.

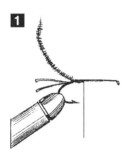

Tie in two strands of rubber to form the setae. Then add a piece of olive chenille (Fig. 1).

Form the abdomen by winding on the chenille, then tie two pieces of legging rubber in crosswise (Fig. 2).

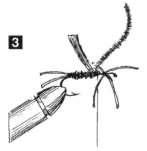

Tie in a piece of the olive-dyed goose wing for the wing cases, followed by another piece of olive chenille, preferably a darker shade than that used for the abdomen (Fig. 3).

Wind the chenille on through the legs to form the thorax, pull over the wing case and finish off the head (Fig. 4).

Before someone points out that insects have six legs I must advise that this pattern is an amputee! All right, put six legs on it if you wish, but the shop-bought ones always seem to have four. Take it from me: trout can't count! Does this Wiggle-Legged nymph work? You bet your best pair of wading boots it does!

BEETLE

MATERIALS

Sproat dry fly hook, Mustad 3904A
  or similar, size 10-14
Chenille, light brown or fawn
Deer hair

Neck hackles, natural red and
  grizzle
Raffine, brown and green

Beetles can be tied and fished as floaters or sinking wet flies. Floaters need plenty of good stiff hackle, while a wet fly uses soft hen hackle.

Chenille makes good beetle bodies but top floating flies are best made with bodies of spun and clipped deer hair.

Wet Fly

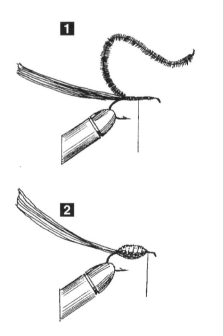

The wet version of this fly is simplicity itself. Start off by whipping the thread along the shank and then tying in a short length of Raffine – brown if it's to be a brown beetle or green for the other option.

Now tie in the end of the chenille – light brown for a brown beetle, or grey for a green (Fig. 1).

Wind the chenille along the shank to form a nice plump beetle-type body. Don't make the body too long. Leave room at the head for finishing off the fly (Fig. 2).

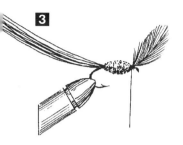

The next step is to tie in a soft hen hackle (Fig. 3).

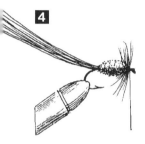

Wind the hackle on, make a couple of turns through it with the tying thread and snip off the end (Fig. 4).

Take the Raffine, pull it forwards and secure by making several tight turns around the head. Trim off the excess, finish off the head, add cement and the fly is finished (Fig. 5).

Floating Fly

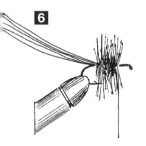

Tie in the Raffine for the wing cases, then spin on some deer hair (Fig. 6). The Basic Techniques section explains this process.

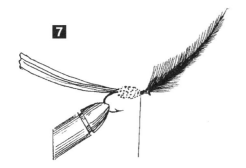

Clip the deer-hair body to shape and tie in a good stiff floating hackle. Use natural red hackle for a brown beetle or a good grizzle hackle if you are tying a green beetle (Fig. 7).

Wind the hackle on, secure with several turns of the thread, then pull the wing case material over, tie it in and clip off the surplus. Finish the head and add cement. You now have a top floating beetle pattern (Fig. 8).

While Raffine is a good shiny material to imitate beetle cases, it is not as durable as some other materials. Turkey tail feather is good for brown beetles and white duck or swan quills dyed green make very passable green beetles.

Some people use strands of bright green lurex, which makes for a very flashy beetle. One thing to remember, though, is that with floating flies, trout see only the undersides and a lot of the flash is lost on them. With a wet pattern however, as it drifts along under the surface, the flash could well mean the difference between fooling a trout and having it ignore your offering.

BLOWFLY PATTERN

MATERIALS

Sproat hook, size 10-12
Lead wire
Bronze peacock herls
Black end of a turkey tail feather

Two grey hackle tips
Soft black hen hackle
Eyes (optional)

This pattern is fished as one would a nymph. During the summer blowflies are often drowned and they drift deep in the river, swirling in the current. The lead wire on the hook helps to take this pattern down into those summer green pools where the trout hang close to the bottom. Let's tie one.

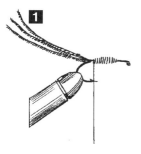

Wind some lead wire onto the hook shank and tie in three peacock herls (Fig. 1).

Now make the abdomen by winding on the herls. If you want to make a sturdier specimen, rib the body with a fine piece of copper wire (Fig. 2).

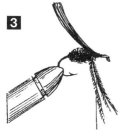

Tie in a piece of the turkey tail (Fig. 3).

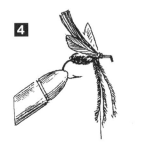

Tie in the tips of two grey hackles. Black hackle points can also be used (Fig. 4).

Next you tie in the black hackle at the head (Fig. 5).

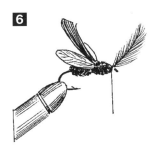

Bring the rest of the peacock herl forward, then wind it on to form the thorax. Secure with the thread and snip off the surplus (Fig. 6).

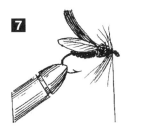

Wind on the black hackle (Fig. 7).

Pull over the piece of turkey feather, tie it in and trim off the excess (Fig. 8).

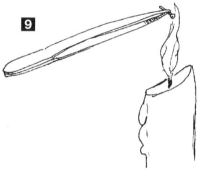

The fly can be finished off at this stage and will be quite effective. However, you may also add black plastic bead eyes, or make them by melting blobs off the end of a short piece of monofilament nylon (Fig. 9).

With the eyes added you have a very realistic-looking fly (Fig. 10).

DEER-HAIR CADDIS

MATERIALS

Sproat dry fly hook, Mustad 3904A,
   size 10-14
Fine gold wire

Hare fur
Grizzle cock neck hackles
Deer hair

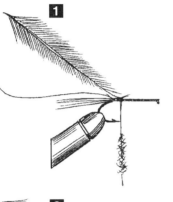

Start off by whipping the hook shank, tying in a tail of bunched cock hackle fibres, the fine gold wire ribbing and a hackle. Twist a pinch of hare fur onto the tying thread (Fig. 1).

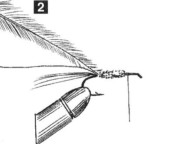

Wind on the body of hare fur (Fig. 2).

Now wind the hackle along over the body and bring the ribbing over it, winding it in the opposite direction to the hackle so that it secures the spine of the hackle feather. Tie in another hackle (Fig. 3).

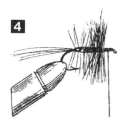

Wind the hackle on (Fig. 4).

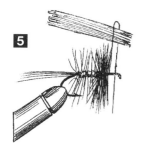

Take a bunch of deer hair, hold it in place and make a couple of careful turns of the thread to put it into place (Fig. 5).

When you are sure that all of the deer hair is sitting on top, and that half of it hasn't slipped around the far side, make some firm tight turns to hold it in place. Trim off the ends, then finish the head (Fig. 6).

Be liberal with the cement, ensuring that it soaks into the butts of that deer-hair wing. Trim the rear end of the wing if it's too long.

A variation of this type of pattern is the **Skittering Caddis**. With this fly, the wing is formed by tying a bunch of deer hair at right angles to the shank (Fig. 7).

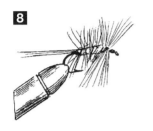

Pull this tight with a series of cross turns of the thread, causing the deer hair to splay (Fig. 8).

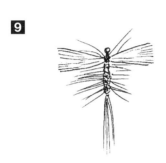

Fig. 9 shows the top view of this pattern.

As the name implies, this pattern is skittered across the surface of the pool to simulate a hatched insect scuttling off to the safety of the rocks and stones along the river's margin.

HACKLE DRY FLY

MATERIALS

Sproat dry fly hook, Mustad 3904A
  or similar, size 10-14

Bronze peacock herl
Cock neck hackles, natural red

This simple dry fly is one of the easiest to tie and it is a truly effective pattern. Some home tiers use hardly anything else, tying this pattern in a variety of sizes.

Tied on a big hook with a plump body of herl it is a good pattern to have when beetles or other terrestrials are on the water. Tied with a slim body, and on a small hook, using only one or two strands of herl, it is useful when mayflies are on the water.

This very handy fly is also the basis of some other popular patterns we will look at.

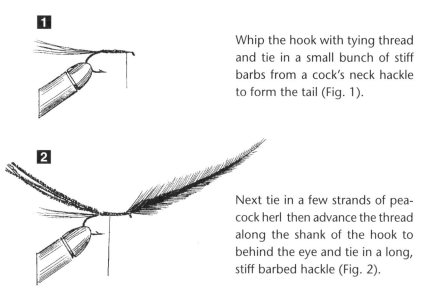

1

Whip the hook with tying thread and tie in a small bunch of stiff barbs from a cock's neck hackle to form the tail (Fig. 1).

2

Next tie in a few strands of peacock herl then advance the thread along the shank of the hook to behind the eye and tie in a long, stiff barbed hackle (Fig. 2).

3

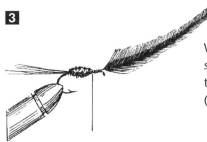

Wind the herl halfway along the shank of the hook and secure with the tying thread. Trim off the ends (Fig. 3).

Take the end of the hackle in the hackle pliers and wind it back along the shank, making close turns until you meet the herl body. Then wind the thread through the barbs of the hackle (about four turns should do), taking care that the points don't become caught under and tied back with the thread.

4

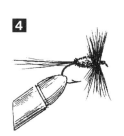

All the barbs should be sticking out from the shank in a regular collar of spikey points. If any are caught under the thread tease them out with the point of a dubbing needle.

Whip the thread to form the head, secure and trim. Put a drop of cement on the head and let it soak back in among the bases of the hackle barbs.

When finishing off the head use the fewest turns possible. You don't want a plump head of tying thread; it should be slim (Fig. 4).

HACKLE POINT WINGED DRY FLY

MATERIALS

Sproat dry fly hook, Mustad 3904A
  or similar, size 10-18
Pinch of blue-grey rabbit fur

Cock neck hackles, grizzle and
  natural red

This is an Adams, a very handy dry fly that suggests some of the members of the mayfly group.

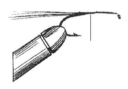

Whip the hook with tying thread and tie in a tail of good stiff barbs from a grizzle cock neck hackle (Fig. 1).

For wings we are going to use small grizzle hackle points. These may be small hackles from the bottom of the cape, which is the top or sides of the bird's head (Fig. 2).
  Alternatively they may be nipped from the top of a longer hackle, the base of which can be saved and used later for hackling bigger flies (Fig. 3).

These two hackle points are then tied along the shank of the hook, tips facing forward. Pull them up and secure in that position by making a couple of turns around their bases (Fig. 4). Make sure they are not too close to the eye.

Now make the body of dubbed fur and tie in a grizzle and a natural red hackle at the head (Fig. 5).

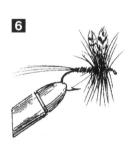

Wind on the two hackles, making sure they are intermingled. Secure them by winding the thread forward through the hackle points. Be careful not to get them tangled with the thread. Use the point of the dubbing needle to pick out any hackle barbs that get caught under.

Whip off and finish the head, then put on a drop of cement, allowing it to soak into the butts of the hackles (Fig. 6).

HOPPER

MATERIALS

Sproat hook 3x long, size 6-10   Cock pheasant tail
Closed cellfoam   Deer hair
Speckled turkey quill

Closed cellfoam, the material used for making trampers' ground mats, is the basis of this pattern. It is cut to shape with a sharp blade or scissors and can be coloured using marking pens.

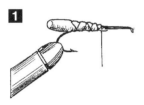

Tie a piece of closed cellfoam onto the hook shank. A careful drop of superglue assists this (Fig. 1).

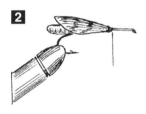

Tie two pieces cut from the speckled wing feather of a turkey one either side of the body (Fig. 2).

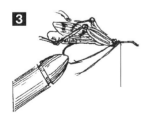

To make the hopper's legs, take two small bunches of strands from the centre tail of a cock pheasant knot them, and tie them in (Fig. 3).

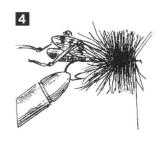

Now spin on some deer hair to fill up the front half of the hook shank (Fig. 4). Trim and clip the deer hair. (See Basic Techniques for instructions on this art.)

Your finished hopper should look like the one in Fig. 5.

The **Cricket** is related to the hoppers but is black. To tie a cricket fly use all black materials and follow the same method (Fig. 6).

IRRESISTIBLE

MATERIALS

Dry fly hook 1x long, size 8-14
Deer hair

Cock neck hackles, grizzle and
    natural red

The Irresistible is a good general pattern: one or two should be in every angler's flybox.

Whip the hook and tie in a tail of grizzle cock neck hackle (Fig. 1).

Spin on some deer hair to fill the rear half of the hook shank (Fig. 2).

Clip the body to shape (Fig. 3).

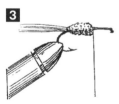

Now tie in two wings of grizzle hackle points (Fig. 4).

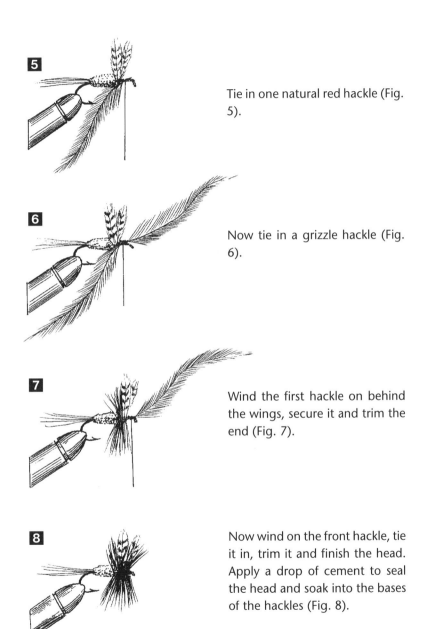

5

Tie in one natural red hackle (Fig. 5).

6

Now tie in a grizzle hackle (Fig. 6).

7

Wind the first hackle on behind the wings, secure it and trim the end (Fig. 7).

8

Now wind on the front hackle, tie it in, trim it and finish the head. Apply a drop of cement to seal the head and soak into the bases of the hackles (Fig. 8).

LACEMOTH

MATERIALS

Sproat dry fly hook, Mustad 3904A
   or similar, size 12-14
Pinch of brown rabbit fur

Grizzle cock neck hackle
Mallard drake's body feather

This is a flimsy little fly, and it has to be tied lightly to be effective. February-March is lacemoth time, when these little vine-hoppers are prevalent in the streamside shrubbery. Many of them end up floating on the water, where the trout queue up to take them as they drift down the current.

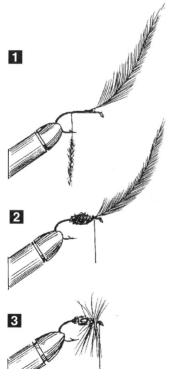

1   Tie in the hackle at the head of the hook and spin a small pinch of rabbit fur onto the tying thread (Fig. 1).

2   Wind the fur onto the hook shank (Fig. 2).

3   Wind on the hackle, secure it with the tying thread and trim (Fig. 3).

4

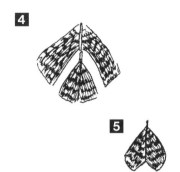

Take a well-marked feather from the breast of a mallard drake and nip out the tip section (Fig. 4).

5

Trim this section to shape (Fig. 5).

6

Lay the prepared wing section on top of the fly body and tie it into place. Trim the stem butt and finish the head (Fig. 6). Cement.

PARACHUTE FLY

MATERIALS

Sproat dry fly hook, Mustad
   3904A, size 10-14
Cock neck hackles

Peacock herl
White calf tail

The parachute style of fly is a very successful type of floater. It especially suggests a mayfly in the spent spinner phase. You can use slightly larger hackles than normal. With the first version I show here, the white calf tail wing becomes the pedestal around which the floating hackle is wound.

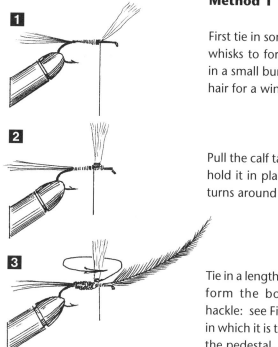

Method 1

First tie in some cock neck hackle whisks to form the tail. Then tie in a small bunch of white calf tail hair for a wing (Fig. 1).

Pull the calf tail wing upright and hold it in place with several firm turns around its base (Fig. 2).

Tie in a length of peacock herl and form the body. Next tie in a hackle: see Fig. 3 for the manner in which it is to be wound around the pedestal.

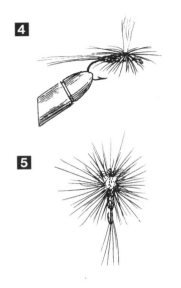

4

Wind on the floating hackle, then tie in at the head and snip (Fig. 4).

5

Add a drop of cement to the head and one at the base of the wing pedestal. This will stop the fly from unravelling and also stiffen the base of the hair wing. From above your fly should look like the one in Fig. 5.

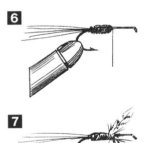

6

Method 2

Tie in the tail and make the body (Fig. 6).

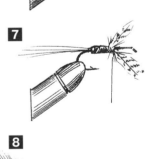

7

Take two hackle points and tie in as wings in the spent position (Fig. 7).

8

Now take a long narrow hackle, cut off the butt end and tie in as illustrated in Fig. 8.

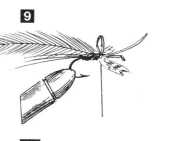

Take the butt up and over in a loop (Fig. 9).

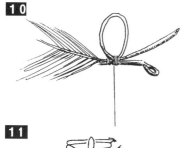

Secure this loop with a couple of firm but not tight turns (Fig. 10). If you tie the butt in too tightly you will not be able to execute the final phase of the operation.

Fig. 11 shows the manner in which the length of the hackle feather is wound around the loop formed by its own butt.

When the hackle has been wound on pull the end of it through the loop (Fig. 12).

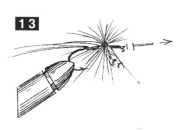

Pull the end of the hackle tight, then the butt of the feather, which projects over the hook eye, is pulled tight. This locks the end of the hackle in the tightened loop. Trim the end of the butt (Fig. 13).

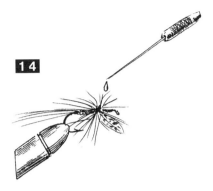

14

Finish off the head and cement it. Apply a drop of cement also on the tightened loop. This will soak into the base of the wound hackle and hold things together (Fig. 14).

15

When viewed from above, your finished fly should look like the one in Fig. 15.

Parachute flies are a neglected branch of the fly tier's art. They are delicate, but they can prove very effective when presented to choosy trout in very clear water.

ROYAL WULFF

MATERIALS

Sproat dry fly hook, Mustad 3904A
   or similar, size 6-16
Brown deer hair
Peacock herls

Scarlet floss
White calf tail
Natural red cock hackle

The Royal Wulff, a good general knockabout fly, has become one of the fly-fishing world's most popular patterns.Used in the larger sizes it is useful when summer terrestrials are on the water, yet it can be tied slim in the smaller sizes and take trout that are feeding on fragile mayflies.

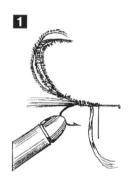

Tie in a bunch of deer hair to form a good float-assisting tail. Then tie in some peacock herls and a piece of scarlet floss (Fig. 1).

The next stage is to tie in a bunch of white calf tail for the wings (Fig. 2).

Form the body by winding on the herls, then make a few turns of the scarlet floss, secure and snip the end off. Make another couple of turns of the herl, tie in and trim (Fig. 3).

The wings are divided by making a few figure eight turns around their bases (Fig. 4).

Then pull the wings upright and take a couple of turns right around the bases (Fig. 5).

Take two hackles and tie them in as shown in Fig. 6.

The one slanting back is wound around behind the wings, tied in and the end trimmed off (Fig. 7).

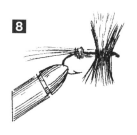

Wind on the second hackle in front of the wings (Fig. 8).

Finish the head and allow a drop of cement to soak into the bases of the hackles and wings.

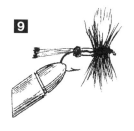

A variation of this popular pattern uses a tail made from golden pheasant tippets (Fig. 9).

TURKEY SEDGE

MATERIALS

Sproat dry fly hook, Mustad 3904A
  or similar, size 10-14
Hare fur
Fine gold wire

Cock neck hackles, natural red
Dark mottled turkey quill or
  grouse tail feathers

The very popular Turkey Sedge represents the adult phase of several members of the caddis fly group.

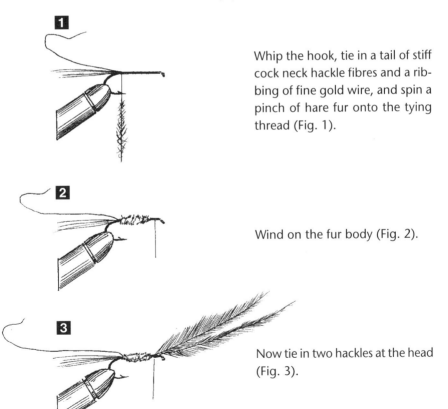

1

Whip the hook, tie in a tail of stiff cock neck hackle fibres and a ribbing of fine gold wire, and spin a pinch of hare fur onto the tying thread (Fig. 1).

2

Wind on the fur body (Fig. 2).

3

Now tie in two hackles at the head (Fig. 3).

4

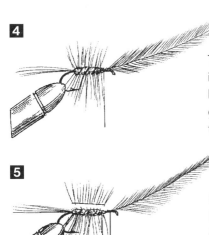

Take one of the hackles and wind it backwards along the body, then hold it in place by winding the gold wire back toward the head to form a rib (Fig. 4).

5

Using the scissors, shear off the hackles along the top of the body (Fig. 5).

6

The next stage is to prepare the wings. One way is to take a section from a turkey quill, paint it with cement and, when it is dried, trim it to shape as shown in Fig. 6.

Another method is to nip the top out of a nicely mottled grouse tail feather (Fig. 7).

The tip section is then stripped on one side, leaving a wing (Fig. 8).

You need a matching pair of these, one from each side of the tip. If you are a dab hand with a scalpel and have a very steady hand it is possible to split the centre stem, giving you the two matching wings from the same feather tip.

7

8

If you use the turkey strip for winging, you will need to fold it along the centre and hold it in place while it is being tied on. The grouse wings are held on and tied in separately. Either way it should look like the one in Fig. 9.

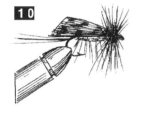

Wind on the other hackle, secure and trim it, finish the head and cement (Fig. 10).

Long-horn Sedge

This insect is the adult of the stick caddis, a grey fly which is especially common on still waters and is readily identified by its long antennae. You can tie excellent copies of this insect by following the Turkey Sedge pattern but tying in horns made from hackle stems from which all the barbs have been stripped. Tie them in just before you tie in the hackles.

For this pattern, use grey duck wing to form the wings. Paint them with thin cement, exactly the same way as for the Turkey Sedge (Fig. 11).

Sedges are very common, especially in spring and early summer, but they are very much a nocturnal insect, becoming active at dusk and well into the hours of darkness. Tie them up in several sizes.

SPENT SPINNER

MATERIALS

Sproat dry fly hook, Mustad
   3904A, size 10-16
Body floss, herl or fur dubbing

Feather material for wing cases
Cock neck hackles

Spent spinners represent the end of the trail for the female mayfly. When egg-laying is finished they drift down the river, dead or dying, spreadeagled on the surface. As they tumble down the rapids they become drowned, drifting along under the surface. Trout love them.

The fly I am about to describe can be either a floater or a wet-type fly. If it stays on the surface that's fine, but if it sinks don't worry. The fly will be behaving exactly the way the natural insect does.

Using this basic pattern as a guide, choose your materials according to the type of spinner you wish to tie. For a spent **Blue Dun** I would use blue rabbit or mole fur for the body,whisks and hackles of blue dun, and hackle points from the same feathers for wings. I would use dark mallard secondary quill feather to make the topping of the thorax.

For a **Red Spinner** or **Dad's Favourite** type of spinner use the materials for that pattern but use natural red hackle points for the wings. And so on! The **Greenwell's**, **Pheasant Tail** and **Twilight** can both be tied this way.

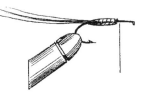

First tie in the tail whisks, then form the abdomen (Fig. 1).

147

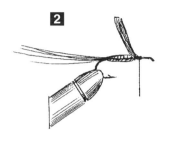

Now tie in the piece of wing quill feather to form the thorax topping (Fig. 2).

Select two hackle point wings. If you are jealously guarding those small fine hackles on that highly prized and expensive cock neck cape, you can make them from the tips of larger hackles by trimming them (Fig. 3).

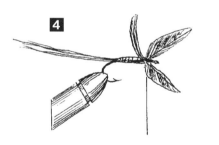

Tie these wings into place (Fig. 4).

Next tie in the hackle at the head of the hook (Fig. 5).

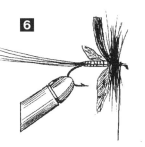

Wind on the hackle to fill up the section of the hook immediately in front of the wings (Fig. 6).

Pull over the topping piece, secure and trim (Fig. 7).

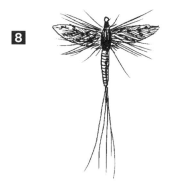

Your finished fly should look like the one in Fig. 8 when viewed from above.

TRADITIONAL WINGED DRY FLY

MATERIALS

Sproat dry fly hook, Mustad 3904A or similar, size 10-18

Cock neck hackles, natural red

Cock pheasant tail strands

Primary feathers from a duck wing

If you have never tried tying this type of fly it would pay to start off using a larger hook. When you have reached a degree of proficiency it's time to accept the challenge of tying number 16s or even 18s.

The pattern I have illustrated here is a version of the Pheasant Tail, a dry fly not as well known as the nymph of the same name but an excellent floating pattern.

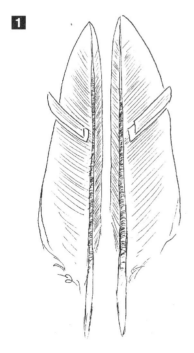

1

We start off by selecting two primary quills from the wings of a mallard duck, one from the right wing and the other from the left. These are 'matched quills' (Fig. 1).

Place them back to back and, using the sharp points of your scissors, snip out two matching pieces of feather. Taken from near the base of the quills they will usually have too much curl, while those from the tip end will be too stiff and thick. The middle section produces the best winging materials. I sometimes use a stout bulldog clip to keep the two quills aligned back to back while I snip out bits of winging feather.

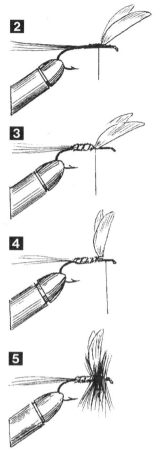

Having selected a pair of wings lay them facing forwards along the hook, which has already had the tail whisks tied in (Fig. 2).

Now tie in the cock pheasant tail fibres and form the body (Fig. 3).

Pull the wings upright and make a couple of firm turns around the base. Put in a drop of cement and let it soak in to help set the wings in the correct position (Fig. 4).

Tie in two stiff floating hackles and wind one of them in behind the wings and the other in front. Secure the thread, tie it off and cement. Behold your finished fly (Fig. 5)!

This method is the basis of all traditional winged dry flies. It can be a complicated business to start off with, but practice soon turns it into a simple affair. Take your time. **Dad's Favourite**, **Greenwell's Glory** and **Twilight Beauty** are some of the patterns tied this way.

To make the smallest versions, your materials all have to be scaled down to an appropriate size. When tying patterns on size 20 and 22 hooks, some tiers actually split the thread to obtain strands thin enough. Duck quill is too heavy for these sizes so blackbird and starling wings are used. When you can turn out these minute flies on the smallest hooks you can really call yourself a fly tier!

WONDER WINGS

This system of winging floating flies is quite ingenious.

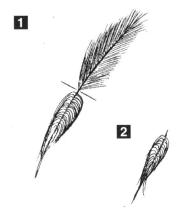

Start off with a large hackle and pull some of the barbs down toward the base of the spine (Fig. 1).

When the piece of hackle is trimmed you are left with a 'wing' (Fig. 2).

Any dry flies can be tied with this style of wing. You tie in a matching pair of wings and complete the rest of the pattern as usual (Fig. 3).

They make excellent wings for large floating patterns such as cicadas (Fig. 4).

A lot of the bigger hackles off a cape can be used up making wonder wings. For regular dry flies the barbs need to be about 20mm long, but for cicadas you will need the biggest hackles on the cape, with barbs at least 30mm long. They can be stiffened by coating them with a layer of thinned-down cement.